Trail Driving Days

TRAIL
DRIVING DAYS

TEXT BY
DEE BROWN

PICTURE RESEARCH BY
MARTIN F. SCHMITT

BONANZA BOOKS · NEW YORK

Contents and Illustrations

CONTENTS AND ILLUSTRATIONS

CONTENTS AND ILLUSTRATIONS

CONTENTS AND ILLUSTRATIONS

CONTENTS AND ILLUSTRATIONS

CONTENTS AND ILLUSTRATIONS

CONTENTS AND ILLUSTRATIONS

CONTENTS AND ILLUSTRATIONS

CONTENTS AND ILLUSTRATIONS

CONTENTS AND ILLUSTRATIONS

CONTENTS AND ILLUSTRATIONS

CONTENTS AND ILLUSTRATIONS

CONTENTS AND ILLUSTRATIONS

CONTENTS AND ILLUSTRATIONS

CONTENTS AND ILLUSTRATIONS

Foreword

The preparation of a book of this kind necessarily requires the cooperation of many persons—photographers, historians, editors, archivists, curators, librarians, collectors, rare book dealers—and in this particular case, ranchers, stockmen, and the descendants of the pioneers who lived this story.

Some of the photographers whose prints are reproduced here are unknown by name; they were itinerants of the new West, traveling across the lonely ranges in their tiny dark-room wagons, or setting up crude studios briefly in boom towns. They caught the cattle roundup outfits in suspended motion around chuckwagons, or they waited in the trail towns for the drivers to come in for posed portraits in new-bought hats, shirts, and boots. The more imaginative photographers attempted to record the cowboy at work and at play, but the cameras of the earliest days were not made for the constant movement of the range rider.

Two men stand out above all others in the photographic records of the open range days. They worked in different geographic areas, Erwin E. Smith in the Southwest, and L. A. Huffman in the Northwest. Huffman began his career about 1878, operating out of Miles City, Montana, recording the great cattle drives into the last free grasslands of Wyoming and Montana during the bonanza days of the 1880's. He was more successful than his contemporaries in capturing wide-sweeping views of the ranges, with men and animals in proper relationship to the backgrounds.

Erwin E. Smith was a Texan who lived most of his life in the ranching country of that state. He worked as a cowboy with the Matador, XIT, LS, JA, L I T, Turkey Track, and other great ranches, carrying a camera and usually a tripod on his saddle so that when the opportunity came for a good picture he made it on the spot, unrehearsed. He tolerated no stilted posing by his cowhand subjects, insisting on absolute naturalism. In 1905, Smith began spending his winters in art schools, studying sculpture for two seasons under Lorado Taft, and then in 1907 enrolling at the Boston Museum of Fine Arts. He told a magazine writer who interviewed him at that time that he would have begun studying art earlier, but had been too busy attempting to record with his camera the workaday lives of real range cowboys before they all disappeared.

Alexander Gardner and William H. Jackson, who are represented by a number of prints, are well known for their pioneer camera work in the early West. After completing his Civil War album, Gardner visited Kansas in 1867, just as the first cattle drives from Texas were coming up the Chisholm Trail; otherwise he would never have been able to show so vividly the trail town life of the period. Some of the Jackson photographs were made during his early survey expeditions in the 1870's, and others are of a later period when he worked for a stationery company in Denver toward the end of the nineteenth century.

Publications consulted are listed at the end of this volume, the great source books being *Historic Sketches of the Cattle Trade,* by Joseph McCoy; *Historical and Biographical Record of the Cattle Industry,* by James Cox; and *Prose and Poetry of the Livestock Industry of the United States.* The outstanding scholarly studies of the subject are *The Range Cattle Industry,* by Edward E. Dale; *The Cattlemen's Frontier,* by Louis Pelzer; and *The Day of the Cattleman,* by Ernest S. Osgood. Paul Wellman's *The Trampling Herd* is a colorful review of the whole industry, and no one has ever matched, as a story of the beginning, the flowering and decline of the open range, James H. Cook's *Fifty Years on the Old Frontier.*

No single volume, however, has told or ever will tell the whole dramatic story of the American cattle trade. One must consult the complete works of such trail blazers as J. Frank Dobie, and the cattlemen's foremost biographer, J. Evetts Haley. To better understand the real cowboy, one must read Charlie

FOREWORD

Siringo and Will James, and that lively vernacular autobiography of Teddy Blue, *We Pointed Them North*. The gunmen who played brief but violent parts in the story have been thoroughly portrayed in *The Album of Gunfighters*, by J. Marvin Hunter and Noah H. Rose. Because of the vastness of the territory involved, details must be filled in by such regional studies as Laura V. Hamner's *Short Grass and Longhorns* for the Texas Panhandle; Ora Brooks Peake's *The Colorado Range Cattle Industry;* and Hermann Hagedorn's *Roosevelt in the Bad Lands,* which not only is a biography but also happens to be an excellent account of early ranching in the Dakotas and eastern Montana.

Deserving of special credits for assistance in collecting materials for this book are Mrs. Opal Harber of the Western History Department, Denver Public Library; Miss Lola M. Homsher, Archivist, University of Wyoming Library; and Miss Helen M. McFarland, Librarian, Kansas Historical Society. Whole sections would be missing had they not been so generous of their time and of their respective collections. We wish to express gratitude also to Henry Biederman, editor of *The Cattleman,* Fort Worth, Texas, who kindly opened his office files to us when we were first beginning this work. His suggestions for further searches saved much time for us.

We are likewise indebted to the following, whose contributions and suggestions helped to close serious breaches in our pictorial narrative: Charles J. Belden; Myrtle D. Berry, Nebraska Historical Society; Earl A. Brininstool; Mary Elizabeth Cody, Wyoming State Library and Historical Department; Mrs. Adolph Colberg; Mrs. C. E. Cook, Oklahoma Historical Society; Caroline Davis, Old Lincoln County (New Mexico) Memorial Commission; Marjorie Douglas, Missouri Historical Society; Joe M. Clark, New Mexico State Tourist Bureau; Mary Kay English, Sedalia (Missouri) Public Library; Gerritt E. Fielstra, New York Public Library; Laura V. Hamner; Helen M. Jackson; C. S. Kingston, Eastern Washington College of Education; Richard M. Long, Wichita (Kansas) *Eagle;* Mrs. Anne McDonnell, Montana State Historical Society; Frederick H. Meserve; Tom Ponting, Tall Weed Stock Farm; A. Williams Postel, U.S. Geological Survey; William G. Reed, Historical Society of New Mexico; Frank Reeves, Fort Worth *Star-Telegram;* Dolores C. Renze, State Historical Society of Colorado; Margaret Rose, State Historical Society of North Dakota; F. C. Taylor, Wichita (Kansas) City Library; Title Insurance and Trust Company, Los Angeles, California; Paul Vanderbilt, Library of Congress; Cody Wade, Jayton (Texas) *Chronicle;* Edward N. Wentworth, Armour's Livestock Bureau.

Acknowledgments are also made to Mrs. L. M. Pettis for permission to use the photographs of her brother, Erwin E. Smith; to J. Frank Dobie for suggestions made and for material used from *A Vaquero of the Brush Country;* to John Clay for permission to use material from his father's book, *My Life on the Range;* to Everett E. Edwards, editor of *Agricultural History* for permission to quote from the diary of William Emsley Jackson; and to the following for material used from publications noted: University of Oklahoma Press, *The Range Cattle Industry,* by Edward E. Dale; Houghton Mifflin Company, *Roosevelt in the Bad Lands,* by Hermann Hagedorn, and *Frontier Trails* edited by Edward E. Dale; Rinehart and Company, *We Pointed Them North,* by E. C. Abbott and Helena H. Smith.

Dee Brown
Martin F. Schmitt

I believe I would know an old cowboy in hell with his hide burnt off. It's the way they stand and walk and talk. . . . Only a few of us are left now and they are scattered from Texas to Canada. The rest have left the wagon and gone ahead across the big divide, looking for a new range. I hope they find good water and plenty of grass. But wherever they are is where I want to go.

—Teddy Blue, *We Pointed Them North.*

CHAPTER ONE

Longhorns and Pioneers

The cattle came over with the Spaniards, two years behind the gold-mad adventurers led by Hernando Cortes. They landed at Vera Cruz in 1521, six heifers and a young bull of sturdy Andalusian stock, sharp-horned fighters fast as wild deer. Gregorio de Villalobos was the first cattleman. He had brought them to Mexico, these offspring of cattle transported first from Spain to Santo Domingo. Accustomed to tropical weather and tropical insects, they grew fat on the steamy coastal grasslands. They increased rapidly in numbers and were joined by other small herds making the sea voyage, and in a decade the tougher ones, the wiry ones with the sharpest-pointed longest horns, were moving north and west.

Twenty years later, Don Francisco Vasques de Coronado was seeing visions of the Golden Cities of Cibola. But as he prepared to march north out of Mexico, he was practical enough to take along some of the progeny of the six heifers and the young bull. Coronado was the first trail driver, with five hundred head of cattle, moving north toward the golden mirage on the high plains. Three centuries later on those same plains where Coronado's visions evaporated, the golden mirage proved true when thousands of cattle herds came driving into the trail towns of Kansas.

During those three centuries, the Longhorns and the cowboys and ranching slowly developed; the Spanish cattle mutating and evolving, the vaquero perfecting his costume and the tools of his trade. The Spanish names still cling, if not in spelling, in pronunciation: chaps, quirt, riata, rancho, sombrero, lasso, corral. And during the three hundred years, the Spaniards became Mexicans, spreading into Texas, seeking more ranching room for their ever-increasing cattle, which served as their main source of food and of leather for boots and saddles. There was always a surplus of livestock, and as the years passed, wild

1

herds of both cattle and horses were roaming over the Southwest—in the grasslands, the sparse brush country, the dry plains, and the rugged mountains.

By the time Texas had won its independence, there was a ratio of six cattle for each Texan. No market existed for beef, but the industrial revolution in the northern United States was creating a demand for hides, tallow, hoofs and horns. The worthless carcasses were usually left to the vultures and the coyotes.

As early as 1842, however, Texans were driving herds of wiry Longhorns into Shreveport and New Orleans. In 1846, while the Texas-Mexico issue was being settled by a national war, an enterprising young man named Edward Piper drove a herd all the way north to Ohio. And when the California gold rush of 1849 created a small but profitable market on the west coast, some Texans moved cattle overland to San Francisco. W. H. Snyder was one of the pioneers of California driving. His outfit followed the Rio Grande north to the continental divide in Colorado, crossed parts of Wyoming, Utah, Nevada, and moved on to San Francisco. It was a two-year operation. Captain Jack Cureton of the Texas Rangers drove eleven hundred Longhorns over the dangerous southern route across New Mexico and Arizona, dodging Apaches all the way. But Cureton figured the drive worth the risks. When he sold his steers to the meat-hungry miners, he took a profit of twenty thousand dollars, a goodly fortune in those days.

The great market, however, lay to the north and east, and among the pioneer trail drivers who pointed the way for the development of the Southwest's great cattle empire was Tom Candy Ponting of Illinois. Ponting's first drive set a record for long distance trail driving that probably was never equaled.

Late in 1852, Tom Ponting and Washington Malone left Christian County, Illinois, for Texas. They were wearing buckskin belts filled with gold to buy steers.

After crossing Missouri and Arkansas, they traveled into the ranching country near Bonham, Texas, and found a place to board with a family named Clutter. "The money we had been carrying around was very heavy," Ponting later recorded, "and it was hard on us, so I took Mrs. Clutter aside and told her our business. This was the first time we had told what our business was. I asked her if she would take the money and put it under her mattress and not mention it to anyone, not even her husband. She promised me she would do so, and we left the money with her, and she kept it safely until we called for it."

When they had gathered about six hundred cattle, Ponting and Malone crossed Red River into Indian Territory and pastured their herd at Boggy Depot. Leaving Malone in charge of the stock, Ponting went to Armstrong's Academy in search of more cattle and chanced to meet there Jesse Chisholm, who a few years later would give his name to the greatest cattle trail of all. Ponting went with Chisholm up the Canadian River to an Indian council. As he found only a few cattle for sale among the Indians, Ponting sought out a rancher named Pussly, who sold him eighty 1200-pound steers for nine dollars a head.

Most of their gold was gone now, and the two cattle driving pioneers headed their herd of seven hundred bawling Longhorns northeast for the Illinois cornfields. They had their troubles on the way. It was a rainy spring, and near Fort Gibson they had to hire Cherokees to help swim the cattle across the Arkansas River; they built rafts to float the supply wagons over. Unfriendly Indians hovered in the vicinity of their night camping spots, trying to start stampedes.

"I sat on my horse every night while we were crossing through the Indian country," said Ponting. "I was so afraid, I could not sleep in the tent; but we had no stampede."

Near Baxter Springs, Kansas, they crossed into Missouri, following the trail to Springfield, where they had their horses shod. "Sometimes while traveling we would forget what day it was and there would be days when we would see no man except those in our company. We would stop at the farmhouses in Missouri and get butter, eggs and bacon. The people did not want to charge us for them, said there was no market for them, and that we were perfectly welcome to them, but we always gave them something, especially if there were any children around."

At St. Louis, they crossed the Mississippi by ferry. "We had hard work to keep the cattle from plunging in the river." On July 26, 1853, they camped for dinner at the old Colony house in Stonington, Illinois, back in Christian County where they had started their journey.

Here the Longhorns got a winter's rest, but in the early spring of 1854, Ponting and Malone selected the best one hundred and fifty of the cattle and started them east, pasturing them every night until they reached Muncie, Indiana. "When we got to Muncie, near the Ohio line, we found we could get cars on to New York. We made arrangements and put the cattle on the cars. Up to this time there had been very little of this work done. We unloaded them at Cleveland, letting them jump out on the sand banks. We unloaded them next at Dunkirk, then at Harnesville, and then at Bergen Hill."

On July 3, 1854, from Bergen Hill in New Jersey, Ponting and Malone ferried their much-traveled Longhorns across the Hudson to New York and took them to the Hundred Street Market, completing a two-year journey of 1500 miles on foot and 600 miles by rail. They were the first Texas cattle to reach New York.

The *Tribune* reported: "The top of the drove are good quality beef, and all are fair. A lot of twenty-one, short eight cwt., sold to Weeks at $80. These cattle are rather long-legged, though fine-horned, with long taper horns, and something of a wild look." The *Tribune* also pointed out the costs of the drive. "The expense from Texas to Illinois was about $2 a head, the owners camping all the way. From Illinois to New York, the expense was $17 a head."

It would be some years, however, before Longhorn beef was commonplace in New York City. The distance and the risks were too great.

Meanwhile in Texas, the cattle continued to multiply. And while most Texans seemed to be raising cattle, a few were trying to find ways to preserve the meat for long distance shipments to the eastern markets. One of the more successful was Gail Borden, who had gained considerable local fame in Galveston by his efforts to invent a land schooner, a covered wagon propelled by a sail. Borden's wind wagon was designed for travelers heading west over the plains. It worked very well, but on a test run dumped its occupants into the Gulf of Mexico. Discouraged, young Borden turned to meat biscuits, which he hoped to sell to the army and navy and to western travelers.

3

When Borden announced he could use one-third of the cattle produced in Texas every year, the cattlemen became interested, and began avidly reading the young inventor's advertising pamphlets. By 1851, he had a meat biscuit factory in operation at Galveston, and the *Galveston News* reported as follows:

"We stepped into this establishment the other day, for the purpose of noting the *modus operandi* whereby beef cattle are converted into biscuit. The arrangements and the machinery are on a much more extensive scale than we had previously imagined, and the whole establishment exhibited a neatness and a cleanliness which we did not expect to see."

Borden's patented process was to boil about 120 pounds of beef down to a molasses thickness of ten pounds and mix it with flour to form biscuits. He won much publicity and a grand prize medal in a London exhibition, but when he lost the army contracts he had hoped for, his packing plant failed. Borden later went to New York and founded the evaporated milk business which still bears his name.

Another Texan who tried to preserve meat was Captain Richard King, who embalmed his beef by infusing the veins with brine. The experiment failed. Consumers wanted fresh meat, not biscuit or embalmed meat. As did Borden, King took another course, and became the first great rancher in Texas.

The story of the King Ranch begins before the Mexican War, when Richard King came to Texas "possessing only a horse, a saddle, and ten dollars in cash." In 1846 he was operating a steamboat on the Rio Grande, hauling American soldiers and supplies to Mexican invasion points. By 1850, King and his partner, Mifflin Kenedy, owned a score of boats, running a profitable cargo business up the Rio Grande from Brownsville. In 1852, while riding with a young lieutenant named Robert E. Lee across the mesquite flats between the Nueces and the Rio Grande, King remarked on the luxuriant grass along the coastland. He thought it would be fine for cattle raising if there were only a market for beef. Lee replied that possibly a market could be found if a man tried hard enough.

Richard King mulled over the idea for a long time, discussed it with Mifflin Kenedy, and then finally bought the Santa Gertrudis tract of 75,000 acres on the Nueces River. He took his savings and began digging wells, buying Longhorns and horses, and hiring an army of Mexican vaqueros. He was so sure of the future, he went down to Brownsville in 1854 and married Henrietta Chamberlain. Six years later the Santa Gertrudis was the major cattle enterprise on the coastal plain, and in 1860 King took Mifflin Kenedy in as a ranching partner. Combining their resources, the two men increased their land holdings and imported Durhams from Kentucky in order to improve their stock.

For them the coming of the Civil War only brought more prosperity, because their boats were in demand for hauling cotton to Brownsville where it was loaded on British merchantmen. By the close of the Civil War, the Running W brand of the Santa Gertrudis roamed over 300,000 acres. In 1868, King and Kenedy halved the ranch between them, but when trail driving finally opened a vast new market, King began to expand again. When he died in 1885, the King Ranch enclosed half a million acres.

Without his steamboat business, however, even Richard King might never have sur-

4

vived the Civil War as a cattleman. Few other Texas cattlemen did last out the war in a state of solvency. Some of them had driven their herds across the Mississippi to supply the southern armies, exchanging their worthless cattle for Confederate money that was also worthless long before Appomattox. Most of the younger men went off to Virginia and Tennessee for four years of fighting. When they returned home, they found their stock scattered in the brush and in the arroyos.

Several weeks after Lee's surrender, Generals Kirby Smith and Joseph Shelby were still leading small bands of unreconstructed rebels in Texas, and there was strong talk of continuing the war from the Southwest.

The majority, however, were weary of war, and even the few who would not surrender and who rode south across the Rio Grande into Mexico knew in their hearts that the fighting was done.

In a final gesture of defiance, they buried the Confederate flag in the great river. This ceremony marked the end of an era, the beginning of a new and exciting period in western history. The Civil War was ended, but for many a year Texans would carry on the feud in Kansas cow towns, baiting the Yankee peace marshals, releasing lusty energies in violent barroom brawls or in sudden explosive gun battles on the streets.

During these same times, the victors to the north were also fitting together the broken pieces of their lives and fortunes. Populations were shifting into cities, but the people wanted meat on their tables—meat formerly obtained in the forests or raised on their farms.

In Chicago a man who had made a fortune selling pork to the Union Army established a packing house. His name was Philip Danforth Armour. One of Armour's packers was an Irishman, Michael Cudahy. A few years later, Gustavus Franklin Swift, a New England Yankee, also read the future correctly and selected Chicago as the future meat center of the earth. They would all play big roles in the development of the western cattle trade.

Christmas Day, 1865, on a 345-acre tract where nine railroads converged, the Chicago Union Stock Yards opened for business. And by early spring of 1866, rumors had reached the Texas cattle country that a steer worth five dollars in useless Confederate money would bring forty dollars in good United States currency in northern markets, such as Chicago.

Like a spontaneous seasonal migration, cattle began moving north from the brush country, the coastal regions, the plains, and the mountains. The Longhorns were there for the taking, unfenced and unbranded. All a man needed were horses, saddles, a few supplies, some good drivers working on shares.

The goals were the nearest railheads, and these were in Missouri. Railroad building, halted by the war, was slowly beginning again, and from Chicago the rails were pushing south and west.

Sedalia, Missouri, was the nearest railroad point for Texans, and in the first warm days of early spring, thousands of cattle from south Texas were driven north along the Sedalia trail, passing Fort Worth and heading for the crossing of Red River. After driving past Denton and Sherman to Red River, crossings were usually made at Rocks Bluff Ford or Colbert's Ferry. The herds then rumbled on through Boggy Depot to Fort Gibson,

5

following approximately the trail used by Tom Candy Ponting thirteen years earlier.

Instead of attacking and scalping, the Indians of the Territory used modern tactics to harass the drivers. They stood on their legal rights by demanding ten cents toll per head of stock, and usually obtained the assessment.

Except for occasional bandits, fierce thunderstorms, unseasonal cold weather, stampedes, and flooded river crossings, the cattlemen had no great difficulty in driving on into Baxter Springs, Kansas. It was here that they encountered real trouble. From Baxter Springs northeastward to the Sedalia railhead, the country was thickly settled with small farmers, most of them recent battlefield enemies of the Texans. They did not want their fences wrecked and their crops trampled.

Some of the settlers also feared Spanish or Texas fever, a fatal cattle disease transmitted by ticks carried on the Texas cattle. The Kansas and Missouri farmers did not then know how the disease was communicated, but they refused forcefully to permit any Southern herds to cross their properties.

And so, thanks to these vigilant Jayhawkers, Baxter Springs became the main cow town of 1866, the first in a series of colorful, sinful trail towns of Kansas.

Over a hundred thousand cattle were dammed up around Baxter Springs through the summer, and occasional violent skirmishes flared between the Confederate Texans and the Unionist Jayhawkers. At last the summer waned. The grass died, or was burned off by the defiant farmers. Dishonest cattle buyers bought herds with bad checks. The unsold cattle died. By autumn, the great spontaneous drive of 1866 was ended. For the Texans it had been a financial bust.

A less optimistic folk might have gone home defeated. But not the cowmen of Texas. By the spring of 1867, many were ready to drive their Longhorns north again.

And in 1867, thanks to an enterprising Yankee stockman of Illinois, a convenient railhead and shipping point would be waiting to welcome their coming.

At the end of the Civil War, Joseph McCoy of Springfield, Illinois, had started a business, buying livestock for resale to the new packing houses in Chicago. McCoy learned of the Baxter Springs debacle from another Illinois stockman, William W. Sugg, who had bought a herd in Texas, driven it north, and had then been caught in the "big bust." It was a doleful tale of lost fortunes.

McCoy realized immediately that good business demanded an open trail from the cattle country to a shipping point on a railroad. His desire to establish a cattle shipping town soon became an obsession, in his own words, "a waking thought, a sleeping dream."

He studied the maps, and early in 1867 went out to Junction City, Kansas, where he tried to interest the local businessmen in building a stockyard. He received no cooperation, but he made up his mind that somewhere on the Kansas plains was the logical place for a railroad cattle shipping point.

Returning to St. Louis, he visited the offices of both the Missouri Pacific and Kansas Pacific* railroads. The president of the Missouri Pacific stared at McCoy's rough unblackened boots, his slouch hat, and wrinkled clothes, and then ordered him out of

* The Kansas Pacific Railroad later became the southern branch of the Union Pacific.

6

the office. The president of the Kansas Pacific was polite enough to listen to his visitor's plans, but was not interested enough to risk any money on the enterprise.

Doggedly, McCoy went back to Kansas, where he was rebuffed also by the leading citizens of Solomon City and Salina. He later recorded that he "was apparently regarded as a monster threatening calamity and pestilence."

But at last, near the end of the rail line of the Kansas Pacific, he found the place he had been seeking. "Abilene in 1867," said McCoy, "was a very small, dead place, consisting of about one dozen log huts, low, small, rude affairs, four-fifths of which were covered with dirt for roofing. . . . The business of the burg was conducted in two small rooms, mere log huts, and of course the inevitable saloon also in a log hut, was to be found."

Abilene, however, met all the requirements for a cattle-shipping town. It was west of the settled farming country. It had a railroad, and a river full of water for thirsty cattle. On the prairies for miles around was a sweeping sea of grass for holding and fattening stock at the end of the drives. And nearby was Fort Riley, offering protection from Indian raids, as well as a potential market for beef.

After McCoy had purchased a tract of land adjoining the town, he settled down to work in earnest. It was already July, and the cattle herds were moving north from Texas. He allowed himself sixty days to construct a shipping yard, a barn, an office, and a hotel.

He arranged for lumber shipments from Hannibal, Missouri, and he wheedled railroad ties from the close-fisted Kansas Pacific in order to build shipping pens sturdy enough to hold wild Longhorns. For the convenience of the drivers and buyers, he built a three-story hotel, naming it the Drover's Cottage.

Meanwhile he had sent his friend, William Sugg, south to meet the cattlemen from Texas and inform them of Abilene, "a good safe place to drive to, where they could sell, or ship cattle unmolested to other markets."

The first herd to arrive was driven from Texas by a man named Thompson who had resold in Indian Territory to a company of cattle buyers, Smith, McCord & Chanler.

The arrival of the second herd was more dramatic. Owned by Colonel O. W. Wheeler of California, it had been assembled in Texas, 2400 cattle and fifty-four cowboys armed for Indian fighting. Leaving San Antonio in early summer, Wheeler headed north, intending to drive to California over the South Pass route. But when the herd reached Kansas, rumors of cholera epidemics and hostile Indian activities alarmed Wheeler's drivers. Wheeler bedded his stock down thirty miles from Abilene, raging like a sea captain faced with mutiny. When he heard of McCoy's shipping pens, he drove into Abilene and sold out.

Other cattlemen began arriving, but the season was late. Not until September 5 did the first shipment move eastward on the Kansas Pacific, and then on to Chicago over the Hannibal and St. Joe Railroad.

One reason for delay was the reluctance of the Kansas Pacific to build a switchline. The railroad insisted on waiting until several herds arrived, and then announced they would build a twenty-car switchline, using cull ties, adding that they expected they would

7

have to take up the tracks the following year. McCoy was so exasperated he held out for a hundred-car line, and finally got it.

Born showman that he was, McCoy aranged for an excursion of Illinois stockmen to come from Springfield "to celebrate by feast, wine, and song, the auspicious event."

When the visitors arrived at Abilene, they found several large tents prepared for their reception, as the Drover's Cottage was not yet ready to open for business. "A substantial repast was spread before the excursionists, and devoured with a relish peculiar to camp life, after which wine, toasts, and speechifying were the order until a late hour at night."

On the following day, "before the sun had mounted high in the heavens, the iron horse was darting down the Kaw Valley with the first trainload of cattle that ever passed over the Kansas Pacific Railroad, the precursor to many thousands destined to follow." Even with the late start, Abilene shipped over 36,000 cattle that first year.

Joseph McCoy wasted no time in preparing for the coming season of 1868. He realized that the most important link to be completed in his plans was a well-advertised route from Texas to Abilene. Upon investigation, he discovered that such a trail was already in existence from Texas across Indian Territory as far north as Wichita.

In 1867 the trail bore no name, but by historic justice it should have been called Black Beaver Trail. Black Beaver, a shrewd old Delaware scout, had used the route in guiding Captain R. B. Marcy's exploring parties and various other expeditions of gold rush days. When the outbreak of the Civil War trapped Colonel William H. Emory's Union forces in Indian Territory, Black Beaver used the same trail as an escape route over which the scout guided the soldiers to safety in Kansas.

As a cattle trail it ran directly south from Kansas for several hundred miles through Indian Territory to Red River and on into Texas.

But the trail was named for a half-breed Cherokee trader, Jesse Chisholm.* In the autumn of 1864, Jesse Chisholm hauled goods over this route south from Wichita and returned in the spring of 1865 with buffalo hides and some cattle. Chisholm retraced his journey in 1865-66, marking the road plainly, and it became known as Chisholm's Trail.

McCoy's contribution to the Chisholm Trail was its extension north from Wichita to Abilene. During the winter of 1867 he sent circulars to every Texas cattleman whose address could be found, extolling the advantages of Abilene as a shipping terminal and inviting the drovers to bring their cattle to his pens. He also sent two agents to Texas to make personal calls on the ranchers, and at the same time he published advertisements in the newspapers of Chicago and other cities, inviting cattle buyers to come to Abilene.

To complete the trail from Wichita to Abilene, McCoy employed a party of engineers to mark the route by throwing up mounds of earth at regular intervals. When this was done he sent his old friend, William Sugg, south to direct herds over the new trail.

---

* Confusion over the origin of the name Chisholm Trail is to be found throughout the history of the cattle trade. In 1866, Thornton Chisholm was trail boss on a drive from Gonzales northwest to Indian Territory and then northeast by way of Topeka into St. Joseph, Missouri. His route was known for a time as Chisholm's Trail. John Chisholm of Paris, Texas, also has been given credit for the origin of the name. And John Chisum of New Mexico gave his name to a "Chisum Trail" in that state. The Chisholm Trail that ended in Abilene, however, was named for Jesse Chisholm. Earliest use of Chisholm Trail in print was probably 1870.

As he was completing every detail to insure a successful cattle shipping season in 1868, a new obstacle arose which threatened disaster to all of McCoy's plans.

A sudden wave of rumors concerning Spanish Fever, and its effects on Longhorns and Texas beef, began spreading across the country. "It was the subject of gossip by everybody," said McCoy, "and formed the topic of innumerable newspaper articles, as well as associated press dispatches. A panic seized upon owners of domestic herds everywhere. . . . The butchers, vendors, and consumers were alike alarmed and afraid to buy, sell, or consume beef of any kind." Several northern and eastern states were considering laws prohibiting importation of Texas cattle or beef.

In the spring of 1868, a considerable delegation of buyers arrived at the Drover's Cottage in Abilene. McCoy anxiously awaited the coming of the cattle. In June they came, long winding herds of Texas Longhorns, splashing across the shallow Smoky Hill River into Abilene. Almost 20,000 were sold in that month.

But in a few weeks 50,000 more had arrived, and the Spanish Fever excitement had killed the market. The buyers departed for Chicago; the Texas drovers began talking of moving their herds elsewhere. McCoy saw his dream collapsing, but he was not beaten yet.

Always resourceful, he suddenly announced a plan that would have done credit to his contemporary, P. T. Barnum. He hired several expert lassoers, led by a Texan named Mark Withers. Then he reinforced a stock car with stout planking, loaded another car with some smart Texas cow ponies, hitched on to a Kansas Pacific work train, and headed west for the buffalo feeding grounds.

Withers and his cowboys went to work, and in two days they had the full-grown buffalo bulls roped and tied. However, they had to spend several more days completing the job of getting the animals into McCoy's reinforced stock car. The buffalo bulls refused to be pushed, coaxed or dragged into the car, and McCoy had to bring out a rope and tackle to haul them abroad.

Long canvas streamers were then hung on each side of the car, and "flaming advertisements were painted in striking colors" proclaiming the wonderful cattle bargains at Abilene. As it rolled through St. Louis on its way to Chicago, the newspapers hailed the progress of the "buffalo train," and upon arrival in Chicago, the buffalo were turned into a grass plot in the Union Stock Yard for public display.

McCoy's clever stunt worked like magic. Chicago buyers came back on a special excursion train, the market revived, and the 1868 season closed successfully. "Indeed," said McCoy, "Texan cattle became suddenly very popular and in great demand."

The following year, Joseph McCoy saw 160,000 cattle pass through his Abilene shipping pens. In 1870, the number rose to 300,000. The Kansas Pacific was kept busy moving the cars, and could scarcely find enough equipment to handle the loads. By this time the Chisholm Trail was worn deep like a river, two to four hundred yards wide, with circular bedding grounds at regular intervals trampled by the passing herds.

By 1870, Abilene boasted ten boarding houses, ten saloons, five general stores, and four hotels. During the summer shipping season, the town was hot, with little swift-turning whirlwinds spinning the powdery dust in the streets. It was noisy with the continual bawling

9

of cattle, the cries of the cowhands, the dust-muffled beat of horses' hoofs. And over all was the pungent odor of the new pine lumber in the buildings of Texas Street, mingling with the jungle smell of the excited animals crowded in the shipping yards by the town.

Texas Street, a prong-shaped thoroughfare running parallel with the railroad, was a double line of false-front buildings, most of them unpainted and graying in the weather. Here were the saloons, the honkytonks, the stores dealing in firearms, boots, hats and horse blankets; here waited the Calico Queens and the Painted Cats, ready to entertain the gallants from Texas.

Rowdiness was increasing, and quarrels mixed with whisky and pistols produced several gunfights. According to Stuart Henry, who was a young boy living in Abilene at this time, "when you heard one or two shots, you waited breathlessly for a third. A third shot meant a death on Texas Street."

Abilene had no law. The leading citizens, including Joseph McCoy, hastened to incorporate the town, pass some ordinances, and build a jail. They posted notices along all the roads leading into town, forbidding the carrying of firearms within the city limits. The cowboys read the notices with interest, and jauntily filled them full of bullet holes.

As soon as the jail was built, a party of celebrating cowhands rode into town and tore it down. It was rebuilt under day-and-night guard, but when a camp cook was incarcerated for being drunk, he was freed in a few hours by his boys. They chased the jailer, broke the lock, and rode away with the cook.

To cool down the celebrating Texans, Abilene employed a marshal on July 4, 1870. His name was Thomas J. Smith, and he took the job at one hundred and fifty dollars a month, with two dollars additional for each conviction of persons arrested by him.

Tom Smith was not a talkative man, but he had learned how to handle street gangs while on the New York City police force. Because of his reputation for breaking up a riot in Bear River, Wyoming, he was called Bear River Tom. A broad-shouldered man with gray-blue eyes and a well-kept mustache, he was quite impressive as he patrolled Texas Street on his gray horse.

Bear River Tom's first act was to post broadsides strategically in the saloons of the town: ALL FIREARMS ARE EXPECTED TO BE DEPOSITED WITH THE PROPRIETOR. His first showdown following this was with a rowdy cowboy called "Big Hank," who was wearing his pistol on the street. When Big Hank refused to disarm, Smith calmly stepped in, struck him a terrific blow on the chin, took his pistol away from him, and ordered him out of town.

News of the bulldozing of Big Hank spread through the cow camps that night, and next morning a man named Wyoming Frank came into town to even the score with Bear River Tom. Wearing two guns, Wyoming Frank sought out the marshal. He received two smashes on his chin. This time, Bear River Tom took one of the challenger's pistols, beat him over the head with it, and told him to leave town and never return.

There were no gun killings during Tom Smith's reign in Abilene, but soon after the cowboys departed in the autumn, a local settler became enraged over a land boundary dispute and ended the marshal's career with a bullet and an ax.

10

EARLY AMERICAN CATTLE

The earliest pictures of American cattle are probably those made by Charles de Granville, a French naturalist who traveled on the western plains during the 17th century. One of de Granville's drawings is shown *above*. Two centuries later, the American plains cattle had become Longhorns, *below*. By the time Texas had won its independence in 1836, there were six Longhorns for each Texan. No market existed for beef at that time, but the industrial revolution in the northern United States was creating a demand for hides, tallow, hoofs and horns.

TOM CANDY PONTING

Among the pioneer trail drivers was Tom Candy Ponting of Illinois, who probably set an all-time record. In 1852, Ponting assembled a herd of seven hundred cattle in Texas and drove them overland to Muncie, Indiana. Here he loaded the cattle on crude railroad cars, and after many stops for feeding and watering finally got them to Bergen, New Jersey. In July, 1854, at the end of twenty-one hundred miles, Tom Ponting ferried his herd across the Hudson River to the Hundred Street Market, the first Texas Longhorns to reach New York City.

TEXAS CATTLE IN NEW YORK

In a few years, Texas cattle became so common on the New York streets, they interfered with traffic. "Through the very busiest part of town they go," said a contemporary journalist, "stopping business, frightening horses, filling eyes, mouths and clothes with dust, stopping travel, getting even into Broadway, and at last reaching the pens or the slaughter-houses on the east side of the town."

12

RICHARD KING

One of the first Texans to recognize the potential fortunes to be made from cattle was Richard King, a steamboat captain on the Rio Grande during the Mexican War. In 1854 he established the headquarters of his famous Santa Gertrudis Ranch, stocking it with horses and Longhorns.

Mifflin Kenedy later joined King in developing one of the cattle empires of Texas, a million acres under the Running W brand.

MIFFLIN KENEDY

MEAT BISCUITS AND WIND WAGONS

Gail Borden, meanwhile, was trying to find a way
to preserve the surplus meat. Borden (*left*) had
already gained considerable local fame in Galveston by his unsuccessful efforts to invent a land
schooner, a covered wagon propelled by a sail.
He now began experimenting with dried beef biscuits, which he sold to gold seekers heading for
Colorado. The gold seekers had more faith in his
biscuits than in his wind wagon, but all of Gail
Borden's efforts made only a small dent in the
Texas meat surplus.

HOME TO TEXAS

The Civil War disrupted the lives of most Texas cattlemen, but in 1865 when they returned from the battlefields to their ranches, they found more Longhorns than they knew what to do with. The cattle were roaming wild; they were grass fat and ready for market. But there was no market.

YOUNG KNIGHTS OF THE CATTLE COUNTRY
(*on facing page*)

Some postwar ranchers amused themselves by playing at jousting, a sport which helped them to forget economic problems. They organized tourneys modeled after those described in Sir Walter Scott's popular novels of the day. Elaborate costumes were designed for the "knights" and "ladies."

PHILIP DANFORTH ARMOUR

In those same times, the victors to the north were also fitting together the broken pieces of their lives and fortunes. Populations were shifting into cities, but the people wanted meat on their tables—meat formerly obtained in the forests or raised on their farms. In Chicago, Philip Danforth Armour read the future correctly and established a packing house.

CHICAGO UNION STOCK YARDS

Christmas Day, 1865, on a 345-acre tract where nine railroads converged, the Chicago Union Stock Yards opened for business.

LONGHORNS ON THE TRAIL

By early spring of 1866, rumors had reached the Texas cattle country that a steer worth five dollars in useless Confederate money would bring forty dollars in good United States currency in northern markets, such as Chicago. Like a spontaneous seasonal migration, cattle began moving north toward the nearest railheads.

SEDALIA, MISSOURI, 1866. (*on facing page, top*)

The nearest railhead for the Texans was Sedalia, Missouri.

FORT WORTH, TEXAS. COURTHOUSE SQUARE IN THE EIGHTEEN-SIXTIES. (*on facing page*)

In the first warm days of early spring, thousands of cattle from south Texas were driven north along the Sedalia trail, passing near Fort Worth and heading for the crossing of Red River. Sometimes the drivers stopped briefly at Fort Worth, which had been a cotton trading center during the Civil War.

18

19

INDIANS DEMANDING TOLL

Instead of attacking and scalping, the Indians of the Territory used modern tactics to harass the drivers. They stood on their legal rights by demanding ten cents toll per head of stock, and usually obtained the assessment. Later it became the custom of cattlemen to pick up strays from other herds and use them for toll payments.

PERILS OF THE TRAIL (*on facing page*)

Except for occasional bandits, fierce thunder storms, unseasonal cold weather, stampedes, and flooded river crossings, the cattlemen had no great difficulty in driving on into Baxter Springs, Kansas.

JAYHAWKERS vs. CATTLEMEN

At Baxter Springs, the trail drivers encountered real trouble. Northeastward to Sedalia the country was thickly settled with new settlers, Jayhawker farmers, most of them recent battlefield enemies of the Texans. Occasional violent skirmishes flared between farmers and cattlemen. The herds were dammed up through the summer by the blockade, many of them dying for lack of grass. Others were sold at a loss. By autumn the great trail drive of 1866 was ended, and for the Texans it had been a financial bust.

JOSEPH McCOY

Joseph McCoy was a cattle buyer for the new packing houses in Chicago. When he heard stories of the Baxter Springs debacle, he realized immediately that the Texas cattlemen must have an open trail from the ranges to a shipping point on a railroad. He went out to middle Kansas early in 1867, seeking a place which would meet his requirements.

ABILENE, KANSAS

He found a place called Abilene, a dozen log huts with a prairie dog town in the middle of a single street. But on the prairie for miles around, there was a sweeping sea of grass.

KANSAS PACIFIC RAILROAD MOVING WEST

Joseph McCoy, the dreamer, could obtain little help from the directors of the Kansas Pacific. The railroad finally agreed to install a switchline at Abilene, but would not risk a cent to help him build his cowtown or his shipping pens. McCoy doggedly went ahead with his plans.

JESSE CHISHOLM (*on facing page*)

Jesse Chisholm, a Cherokee trader, had already marked a trail suitable for driving cattle north across Indian Territory into central Kansas. Along this route in 1867, Joseph McCoy sent agents to direct the cattlemen into Abilene. From the beginning it was known as Chisholm's Trail.

ABILENE LOADING PENS

Meanwhile McCoy was busy as a beaver in Abilene, rounding up heavy planking and railroad ties to construct sturdy shipping pens and loading facilities for the expected herds of cattle.

"THEN WE ROUNDED 'EM UP, AN' WE PUT 'EM IN CARS, AN' THAT WAS THE END OF THE 'BAR-C-BARS'" (on facing page, top)

In spite of McCoy's energetic efforts, Abilene in 1867 was a poor cowtown. Not until September 5 did the first shipment of cattle move eastward on the Kansas Pacific and then on to Chicago over the Hannibal & St. Joe line. Born showman that he was, McCoy persuaded a group of Illinois stockmen to come out for the festive occasion. But with the late start, Abilene shipped only thirty-six thousand cattle that first year.

LOADING BUFFALO (on facing page)

In 1868, prejudice against Longhorns, because of the spread of Texas Fever, almost destroyed Abilene as a trail town. But McCoy was equal to the occasion. He hired an expert with the lariat to capture a carload of buffalo, then covered the car's sides with lurid streamers advertising twenty-five thousand cattle for sale in Abilene, and sent it rolling into Chicago. The wild buffalo were a sensation, and Illinois buyers responded by rushing to Abilene to buy the unsold cattle.

KANSAS CITY STOCKYARD, 1872.

Kansas City was the point where the Kansas Pacific railroad unloaded cattle from the west for feeding and watering before shipment to Chicago. Local citizens lost no time in building a stockyard to handle the business. Buyers on fence in photograph *above* are inspecting a pen of varicolored rangy Longhorns.

WHEN ABILENE WAS WILD

By 1870 Abilene boasted ten boarding houses, ten saloons, five general stores, and four hotels. Texas Street was a double line of false-front buildings, most of them unpainted and graying in the weather. Here were the saloons, the honkytonks, the stores dealing in firearms, boots, hats, and horse blankets. Here waited the Calico Queens and the Painted Cats, ready to entertain the gallants from Texas.

"BEAR RIVER" TOM SMITH

To cool down its celebrating visitors, Abilene built a jail. When the cowboys tore it apart, the town appointed Thomas J. Smith as marshal. He was a veteran pacifier of New York street gangs, and knew how to keep Abilene quiet. The cowboys called him "Bear River Tom."

CHAPTER TWO

Cattle, Horses and Men

As trail driving developed into a major activity in the Southwest, the work of rounding up cattle and getting them to market gradually became routinized. But in the early years, it was more like a hunt than a cattle roundup.

The wild Longhorns hid in the brush and chaparral, and had to be pulled out by force, or lured out with tame cattle decoys. James H. Cook, a trail driver who later became one of the great cattlemen of the West, has described a wild Longhorn roundup.

"We went about five miles from the home ranch and camped near an old corral. The corrals in that country were all made about alike. A trench some three feet deep was dug in the ground. Strong posts about ten feet long were then placed on end, closely together, in these trenches, and the ground tramped firmly about them. They were then lashed together about five feet above the ground with long strips of green cowhide. . . . The following morning about sunrise we left the corral, taking with us the decoy herd."

As soon as wild cattle were observed in a dense clump of chaparral and mesquite, the roundup crew led the decoys into the brush, surrounded the place, and began singing a peculiar melody without words.

"A few minutes later," said Cook, "some of the cattle came toward me, and I recognized a few of them as belonging to the herd which we had brought from our camp. In a few seconds more I saw that we had some wild ones, too. They whirled back when they saw me, only to find a rider wherever they might turn. The decoy cattle were fairly quiet, simply milling around through the thicket, and the wild ones were soon thoroughly mingled with them."

It was an easy matter to drive the mixed herd into the corral, but several days were required to bring the wild Longhorns under control for a trail drive. They were usually left in the corral until they were so hungry that grass appealed to them more than flight.

Other methods were used to capture Longhorns in the open. Moonlight nights were

31

considered favorable times for rope hunting, and when caught the cattle were tied down by all four feet. Next day tame cattle would be driven out and the wild ones released among them. "If they had been left for several hours, their legs would be so benumbed and stiffened that they could not run fast. . . . Sometimes when regaining their feet they would charge at the nearest live object and keep right on through the bunch of cattle and line of riders. It would then be necessary to rope and throw them again."

In a few years, however, range cattle became accustomed to seeing mounted cowboys. An outfit of good riders on fast cow ponies could gather a herd in relatively smooth fashion.

The success of a roundup usually rested largely upon the shoulders of the range boss, who in the early days was the ranch owner. As big ranching developed, the owner would select an experienced and respected cowhand for the job. During a roundup, the authority of the range boss was as ironclad as that of a ship's captain, but to keep his job he had to know how to manage three of the most unpredictable members of the animal kingdom— cattle, horses, and men.

Roundups for assembling a trail herd were begun early in the spring, with every cattleman eager to hit the trail first in order to insure plenty of grass along the route to Kansas. At the beginning of a "gather," the roundup boss would assemble an outfit of about twenty cowhands, a horse wrangler to look after the mounts, and, most important of all, a camp cook.

On range or drive, the chuckwagon was home, and a good cook was supposed to be proficient at more than the culinary arts. He had to be a combination housekeeper, morale builder, and expert wagon driver or "bull whacker." The cowhands usually referred to the cook as the "Old Lady," but they were careful not to offend him. He had too many subtle ways of evening the score. The cook was the aristocrat of the roundup and trail drive, a man who prized his dignity, was seldom a good rider, and had slight use for the temperamental cattle.

As for the chuckwagon, it was a work of utilitarian art, an invention of a master cattleman, Charles Goodnight.* The chuckwagon was a commissary on wheels, a stout wagon covered with canvas and equipped with a box at the rear for storing tin dishes, a Dutch oven, a frying pan, kettle, and coffee pot. The standard staples also had their exact places: green-berry coffee, salt pork, corn meal, flour, and beans. For fresh meat, of course, there was always plenty of beef handy. A folding leg was usually attached to the chuck box lid, so that it formed a table when lowered for action. The main body of the wagon was packed with bedrolls, slickers, extra clothing. Fastened securely in the front was a water barrel with a convenient spigot running through the side of the wagon. Beneath the bed was a cowhide sling for transporting dry wood, kindling or buffalo chips. And in a box below the driver's seat, the cook usually kept necessary tools such as axes, hammers, and spades.

The first day of a roundup, the men would be up before dawn to eat their breakfasts hurriedly at the chuckwagon, and then in the graying light they would mount their best ponies and gather around the range boss for final instructions.

* See Chapter Five for the story of Charles Goodnight.

32

As soon as he had outlined the limits of the day's roundup, the boss would send his cowhands riding out in various directions to sweep the range. When each rider reached a specified point, he turned back and herded all the cattle within his area back into the camp center. All day the men worked the animals back, seeking them out in brush thickets and in arroyos. By evening a restless, noisy herd would be assembled beside the camp. As darkness fell, the cattle usually quieted and gathered close together to rest or sleep on the ground, and the roundup boss assigned night herders to hold the herd in place by patrolling its borders.

After supper in a cow camp, while the cook was washing the pots and pans, the cowboys who were free of duties liked to assemble around the fire for some singing. If they were lucky, a fiddler would be among them. They sang rollicking songs, sad songs, unprintably ribald songs, but usually ended with a sacred hymn. Soon afterward, all except the night herders would be in their bedrolls; the next day's work would begin before the sun was up.

The second operation of a roundup began as soon as a herd had been collected. This next step was to separate from the herd the mature animals which would be driven north to market, and the calves which were to be branded for return to the range.

"Cutting out," it was fittingly called, and this performance was, and still is, the highest art of the cowboy. Cutting out required a specially trained pony, one that could "turn on a dime," and a rider who had a sharp eye, good muscular reflexes, and who was an artist at handling a lariat.

After selecting an animal to be separated from the herd, the rider and his horse would begin an adroit game of twisting and turning, of sudden stops and changes of pace. Range cattle were adept at dodging, and if a cowboy's pony was not a "pegger" the chased animal would soon lose itself in the herd. Some horses never learned the art of cutting out; others seemed to sense instinctively what was demanded of them. For the latter the work was pure sport and show. Working with the best type of cutting pony, a cowboy could drop his reins over the saddle horn and by pressure of a knee indicate the cow he wanted, leaving the rest of the action to his mount.

If calves were being cut out, the objective was usually the mother cow. The calf would follow her out of the herd into the open where it could be roped with ease.

Roping, the final act of the cutting out process, also required close cooperation between pony and rider. As soon as a steer or calf was clear of the herd, the cowboy lifted his coiled lariat from its place beside the saddle horn, quickly paid out an oval-shaped noose six or seven feet in diameter, and spun it out over his head with tremendous speed. An instant before making the throw, he would draw his arm and shoulder back, then shoot his hand forward, aiming the noose sometimes for the animal's head, sometimes for its feet.

As the lariat jerked tight, the rider instantly snubbed it tight around the saddle horn. At the same moment, the pony stopped short, practically sitting down. The position of a pony at the moment of the throw was important; balance in motion is a delicate thing, and a sudden jerk of a taut lariat could quickly spill horse and rider.

33

Forefooting was found to be particularly effective with calves, the noose catching the animal by the feet and spilling it in a belly slide, with no damage done. If roped around the neck, a lusty calf would usually have to be forced to the ground, by "bulldogging" it. Bulldogging is a sort of cow *jiujitsu,* and as seen today is a more modern technique than was used in trail driving days. Old-time "doggers" used no ropes, but were clever enough to select fast-moving animals for their victims. By throwing one arm over a calf's head and quickly twisting its neck, an experienced cowhand could unbalance the animal and drop it to the ground like a surprised wrestler—if it was moving swiftly enough.

Tail-twisting was sometimes an effective method of downing calves, and some of the tougher breed of cowboys thought nothing of grabbing a full-grown Longhorn by the tail, twisting the appendage around a saddle horn, and dumping the luckless animal to the ground. But most working cowboys preferred ropes, leaving bulldogging and tail-twisting to rodeo exhibitionists.

As soon as an unbranded animal was roped, it was immediately dragged or herded to the nearest bonfire, where the branding irons were being heated to an orange red. In Texas, all branding was done in a corral, a legal requirement devised to prevent hasty and illegal branding by rustlers on the open range.

Branding, the heraldry of the range, is as old as Spanish-Mexican cattle ranching. When he established a ranch in Mexico, Don Hernando Cortes started the practice by searing three crosses on the flanks of each of his cows. The first brands in Texas were usually the initials of the owner, and if two cattlemen had the same initials, a bar or a circle distinguished one from the other.

During the Mexican War, while most of the Texas ranchers were too busy with other matters to attend to their stock, many cattle reached maturity without being branded. Colonel Samuel A. Maverick owned such a herd near San Antonio. Maverick had taken four hundred cattle as payment for a debt in 1847, and had them delivered to his place on Matagorda Peninsula. As his duties kept him in San Antonio, he had no time to look after the cattle, which multiplied rapidly on the tall grass of the Peninsula, and were as wild as antelopes. So many strayed to the mainland unbranded, that when ranchers in the coastal area saw an unmarked Longhorn, they would say: "That's one of Maverick's," or "That's a Maverick."

As no effort was made to retrieve the strays, other cattlemen picked them up and branded them. Finally, Samuel Maverick received an anonymous note from the Matagorda area: "Send someone to look after your stock of cattle immediately or you will not have in 18 months from this time one yearling nor calf to 10 cows."

In 1853, Maverick sent down a party of cowboys and they managed to round up approximately the same number as had been put on the Peninsula six years earlier. They were driven up to a ranch near San Antonio, while Maverick sought out a buyer for them. He had had enough of absentee cattle ranching.

At last he found a buyer, Toutant Beauregard of New Orleans. The cattle were so wild, however, that Monsieur Beauregard never caught all of them. For years, some of the "mavericks of Matagorda" wandered about the plains of southern Texas, and so was

34

created a new word in the American language. To this day any unbranded adult range cow is known as a maverick.

In the early years, friction over unbranded cattle caused many a gunfight. Brand artists could alter marks, easily changing a "C" to an "O"; and "F" to an "E"; a "V" to a "W." Or for example, JY into OX. By ingenious use of triangles, diamonds, and squares, almost any brand could be changed to suit a rustler's convenience.

Brand blotchers frequently used a running iron, shaped like a poker and used like a pencil. When most states made possession of a running iron illegal, they substituted broken horseshoes, riding bits, or baling wire. The latter was especially favored because it could be easily twisted to effect any sort of brand desired. To make the changed brands look like old markings, the clever rustlers used wet blankets between the hot wire and the stolen animal's hide.

Public registration of legitimate brands was soon established by law, however, so that cattlemen could detect a blotched brand. In Texas, brands were recorded by counties; other States had State brand books.

As additional identification, ranchers also branded their cattle with earmarks. An ear cut squarely off was called a crop. A nick on the upper edge was an over bit. A nick on the lower edge was an under bit. An angling crop on the upper edge was an over slope. An angling crop on the lower edge was an under slope. A triangular piece cut from the tip was a swallow fork, and the ear split deep was the jingle bob.

Ranchers vied with each other in designing unusual brands, preferably brands which would be difficult to change. Some memorable brands were the Hash Knife, the Bible, the Stirrup, the Dinner Bell, the Andiron, the Scissors, the Buzzard on a Rail, the Hog Eye, Turkey Track, Ox Yoke, Frying Pan, and Pancho Villa's remarkable Death's Head. John R. Blocker designed for himself the Block R. John Chisum preferred a straight bar, calling it the Long Rail, and he also used the Jingle Bob ear mark. After winning some large stakes in a fast poker game, Burk Burnett designed his famous Four Sixes, incidentally one of the most difficult brands to alter.

Range heraldry might be romantic, but for the cowboy the operation of branding was his toughest and roughest job. Getting a hot iron on a stubborn cow or calf, whether in the open or in a corral, was never easy or pleasant work. When dragged to the branding fire even the mildest mannered animal would begin bawling and kicking. The continual dust almost suffocated the struggling cowboys, and over everything was the acrid smell of burned hair and hide.

A technique was early developed whereby two men known as flankers tackled from opposite sides. One doubled up the animal's front leg and put his knee on its head. The other flanker braced one of his feet against the animal's hind leg, stretching the other to full length. The brander then pressed the hot iron home, and the checker entered another mark in the roundup tally book.

As soon as the work of branding was completed, preparations for the trail drive would begin in earnest. One of the first things to be done was to acquire a plenitude of horses. Wild horse herds were the usual source, and they were rounded up much like the wild Longhorns, although mustangs were much more difficult animals to tame.

Each cow waddy going up the trail had to have six to ten mounts, because horses, like men, possess varied qualifications. One might be superior at cutting out, but inferior at night herding; another might be excellent for work around a cow camp, but poor on the range or drive. And on a long drive, with no grain for feed, mounts had to be changed frequently so that they could be kept in good riding condition on their diet of wild prairie grass.

Wild horses not only had to be corralled and branded, they had to be broken to the saddle and bridle. The process was sometimes rough on both horses and men. In the early years of the range, quirts and spurs were freely used.

Even after a good breaking in, some high-spirited horses just naturally were offended by saddles and bridles. A back fall or roll was one method they used to shake off riders. But a good cowman did not object to spirit in his mount. He knew a lively actor made the best cow pony and could be gentled with the right sort of training.

The horse herd accompanying a trail drive was known as the remuda (pronounced *remoother* in Texas). From a hundred to a hundred and fifty horses formed the average drive's remuda, and they were handled by a young waddy known as the horse wrangler. The wrangler was usually a young boy, the job being considered more or less as an apprenticeship for trail driving. He was the butt of many a cowhand's joke, and always had to ride the poorest horse in the remuda. But the wrangler was responsible for every horse in the herd, and was supposed to know their individual traits and habits.

When the riders selected their mounts for the day, a temporary corral was usually made by the wrangler and two or three cowboys who held a long rope a few feet off the ground. This kept the remuda in place until the men could rope and saddle their horses. Trained cow ponies had great respect for ropes, and the best ones would stand in position through a long session at the chuckwagon if their riders merely dropped the bridle reins on the ground in front of the horses' feet.

As the day for the trail drive approached, each cowboy assigned to make the trip would busy himself at gathering his personal gear for the journey. In describing his first trail drive, James H. Cook says: "When Mr. Roberts informed me that I was to be one of his trail waddies, I immediately moved all my personal belongings over to his camp. I was allowed to take five of the best saddle horses which I had been riding, to be used on the trail. Robert's trail crew consisted of twelve riders and the cook, besides myself. . . .

"On the trail we were each allowed to take a pair of bed blankets and a sack containing a little extra clothing. No more load than was considered actually necessary was to be allowed on the wagon, for there would be no wagon road over most of the country which we were to traverse, and there was plenty of rough country, with creeks and steep-banked rivers to be crossed. We had no tents or shelter of any sort other than our blankets. Our food and cooking utensils were the same as those used in cow camps of the brush country. No provision was made for the care of men in case of accident."

Although Cook does not describe the clothing he wore, it is certain that every item was designed for utility. And because of its basic practicality, the working cowboy's cos-

36

tume has changed very little in almost a century. He seldom wore a coat because it retarded freedom of movement, and if he wore a vest he rarely buttoned it because he believed that to do so would cause him to take a cold. He wore chaps, not to be picturesque, but to protect his legs from underbrush and weather.

He wore high heels on his boots to keep his feet from slipping through the stirrups, and gloves, not for vanity, but because the toughest palms could be burned raw by the lariat he used constantly in his work. He paid good money for a good-sized hat because it was his roof against the elements; he wanted it big like an umbrella to keep off the sun, the rain and the snow.

As for the bandanna, J. Frank Dobie once proposed that it be made the official flag of the range country, and he has catalogued some of its uses: To protect the back of the neck from the sun; for a dust mask; an ear cover in cold weather; a towel; a blindfold for skittery horses; for tying a calf's legs together while branding it; as a strainer when drinking muddy water; a dish dryer; a hat tie in windy weather; a sling for broken arms; a bandage; as an aid in hand signaling; a face covering for dead cowboys; for hanging horse thieves.

Getting the average trail herd of three thousand cattle underway was as complicated an operation as starting an army on a march across country. The personnel consisted of sixteen to eighteen cowboys, a cook and his wagon, and a horse wrangler for the remuda. As a trail herd usually consisted of cattle from several owners or ranchers, a uniform road brand was sometimes applied. This task was much simpler than regular branding, the cattle being driven through a chute. A light application of the hot iron was pressed on each animal as it moved past the branders.

In the early days, the cattle in a trail herd were a mixed lot—varicolored Spanish cattle with small short horns; brown west Texas cattle with slight stripes down their backs and long shiny blue horns; and the Texas Longhorns, ungainly white-patched animals with half-twisted backs, gaunt bodies and narrow hips. At the start of a drive they were always jumpy.

To keep a herd in order, the wise trail boss searched out a huge dominating animal and made it the lead steer. Charles Goodnight had one called "Old Blue," a veteran of several drives from the Panhandle to Kansas. After a day or so on the trail, barring an early stampede, the cattle would fall into place each morning like infantrymen on the march, each one keeping the same relative position in file as the herd drifted northward.

It was necessary to move slowly at first until the cattle were accustomed to the routine of the drive. When camp was broken in the early morning, the herd was not pushed but was allowed to graze if sufficient grass was on the trail. In the order of movement, the trail boss rode two or three miles in advance, seeking a watering place for the noon camp. Behind him was the chuckwagon driven by the cook, with the horse wrangler and the remuda on the left or right. Then came the point with the lead steers in front and the point riders on the sides, and strung along the widening flow of the herd were the swing and flank riders.

John Clay, a Scotsman who became one of the great ranchers of the West, has left a classic description of a trail herd in movement: "You see a steer's head and horns silhouetted against the skyline, and then another and another, till you realize it is a herd. On each flank is a horseman. Along come the leaders with a swinging gait, quickening as they smell the waters of the muddy river."

The tail or drag riders brought up the rear, the least desirable position on a drive. The drag riders had to keep the lame and weak cattle moving, and all day they rode in clouds of dust, assailed by the generated heat and smells of the herd. Beginning cowboys usually received this assignment, and as they achieved experience and seniority, they moved up toward the point on later drives.

During a day's march, a herd would average about fifteen miles progress. Each evening the herd had to be bedded down, and the night watch assigned, the men usually working in shifts of two to four hours. That most dreaded occurrence of a trail drive, a stampede, usually originated at night. Sometimes a sudden noise, the crackling of a dry twig, the rattle of a cook's skillet, would set the whole herd into mad flight.

To keep the restive cattle quiet, the night watch rode slowly around the herd, crooning to the animals—*Dinah Had a Wooden Leg, Hell Among the Yearlin's, Saddle Ole Spike, Cotton-Eyed Joe, Sally Gooden, The Dying Cowboy.* When weary of singing the same old songs, the night herders invented new verses, sometimes chanting with deep religious fervor a string of disconnected profanity, or the text from a label of Arbuckle's coffee, or perhaps an unflattering original discourse on the habits of Longhorns.

The cowboys soon learned that cattle liked slow mournful songs, the sadder the better, which may account for the dolorous quality of so many cowboy ballads.

As on the range, the cowboy's life on the trail revolved around the chuckwagon. First man up in the morning was the cook. After shaking the dew from the canvas which covered his kitchen on wheels, and firing up with buffalo chips, his raucous voice would awaken the sleeping cowboys: "Arise and shine! Come and get it!" Shivering in the cold of the prairie dawn, they would rise from their blankets, pull on their boots, and stumble toward the comforting smells of the chuckwagon. Or perhaps the cook had his own variation of a formula used by a certain celebrated trail driving sourdough artist: "Come, boys, get up and hear the little birds sing their sweet praises to God Almighty; damn your souls, get up!"

Chuck times were the best times of the day, even though food on the trail seldom varied. Black coffee, sourdough biscuit, beans, meat and gravy. A delicacy was fresh onions, which they could find growing wild as they drove across the Indian Territory into Kansas in late spring.

Except for the short periods of delight offered by the cook and chuckwagon, the trail riders had little time for relaxation. At odd moments there might be a game of seven-up or poker, customarily played for matches on the trail, because there would be no money in their pockets until they reached a shipping town.

But to enliven the daily routine, each outfit usually had at least one practical joker, such as Tommie Newton, who rode with the J. W. Simpson herd. On one drive, Tommie Newton was the only cowboy along who had ever crossed Red River, and when the herd neared that stream, he rode ahead to scout a crossing. For once, he found that treacherous river's waters quite low, with white sand bars glittering in the sun. But at a distance, the stream appeared to be on a wild rampage, and Tommie Newton told the boys it was.

"Better shed your clothes and six-shooters right now," said he, "and put 'em in the chuckwagon. I'll go ahead with the cook and wagon and cross on a ferry boat around the bend."

Dutifully, the boys removed everything but their hats and long drawers. Then Tommie Newton and the cook drove off with the wagon and all the outfit's clothing, and crossed Red River with the greatest of ease. After ordering the cook to drive on a couple of miles, Tommie waited on the north bank, listening with keen delight to the profanity of the cowboys in their long underdrawers as they drove that herd across the Red River sand bars.

But for the most part, trail driving was a tough, dangerous business, a time of unending tension for the trail boss, a time of almost continual weariness and danger for every driver. The weather and the Indians were constant threats. A violent thunderstorm or a party of beef-hungry braves waving blankets could start a stampede in a matter of seconds, and to a cowboy on the trail, the cry of stampede connoted more terror than any other sound in the language.

One of the few trail drivers to keep a diary en route was George Duffield, who drove a herd of about a thousand Longhorns from southern Texas to Iowa in 1866. Stampedes and weather made life miserable for Duffield and his outfit all the way up the trail.

On May 1st he recorded: "Big Stampede. Lost 200 head of Cattle." May 2nd: "Spent the day hunting & found but 25 Head. It has been Raining for three days. These are dark days for me." May 3rd: "Day spent in hunting Cattle. Found 23. Hard rain and wind. Lots of trouble."

By May 8th, they were ready to travel again. "Rain pouring down in torrents," says Duffield. "Ran my horse into a ditch & got my Knee badly sprained—15 miles." May 9th: "Still dark and gloomy. River up. Everything looks *Blue* to me."

On May 14th, a crossing of the Brazos was attempted. "Swam our cattle & Horses & built Raft & Rafted our provisions & blankets &c over. Swam river with rope & then hauled wagon over. Lost Most of our Kitchen furniture such as camp Kittles Coffee Pots Cups Plates Canteens &c &c."

Next day things went badly again. "It does nothing but rain. Got all our *traps* together that was not lost & thought we were ready for off. Dark rainy night. Cattle all left us & in morning not one Beef to be seen."

May 16th: "Hunt Beeves is the word—all Hands discouraged. & are determined to go. 200 Beeves out & nothing to eat." May 17th: "No Breakfast. Pack & off is the order. All hands gave the Brazos one good harty damn & started for Buchanan."

Finally they reached Red River, on May 31st: "Swimming Cattle is the order. We worked all day in the River & at dusk got the last Beefe over—I am now out of Texas—This day will long be remembered by me—There was one of our party Drowned today."

June 1st: "Stampede last night among 6 droves & a general mix up and loss of Beeves. Hunt Cattle again. Men all tired & want to leave."

June 2nd: "Hard rain & wind Storm. Beeves ran & I had to be on Horse back all

Night. Awful night. Men still lost. Quit the Beeves & go to Hunting men is the word—4 P. M. Found our men with Indian guide & 195 Beeves 14 Miles from camp. Allmost starved not having had a bite to eat for 60 hours. Got to camp about 12M. *Tired.*"

All the way to Fort Gibson, the story was one stampede after another. And by this time the Indians were making trouble. On June 18th, however, Duffield recorded one pleasant event: "Cook dinner under a tree on the A K [Arkansas] River Bank with two Ladies." He does not say who they were, but they must have been guests from the fort.

Next day: "15 Indians came to Herd & tried to take some Beeves. Would not let them. Had a big Muss. One drew his Knife & I my Revolver. Made them leave but fear they have gone for others."

After crossing the Arkansas on June 27th, Duffield wrote: "My Back is Blistered badly from exposure while in the River & I with two others are suffering very much. I was attacked by a Beefe in the River & had a very narrow escape from being hurt by Diving."

A month later the herd was still in Indian Territory, after driving into Baxter Springs and then turning back to cross Kansas farther west. July 26th: "The day was warm & the Flies was worse than I ever saw them. Our animals were almost ungovernable."

Duffield's drive ended October 31st, when he reached Ottumwa, Iowa, and sold what remained of the herd. He had less than five hundred of the original thousand cattle that started from Texas six months earlier.

As drivers gained experience on the trail, they learned ways to prevent stampedes. Quite often the cause of a series of stampedes was a single jumpy animal, and if such an individual was spotted it was immediately killed and the meat turned over to the cook. Charlie Siringo says that at the beginning of a drive his outfit tied the hind legs of the worst offenders. "Sometimes we had to sew up the eye-lids of these old 'Mossy-horn' steers to prevent them running for the timbers every chance they got. It required about two weeks time to rot the thread, allowing the eyes to open. By this time the animal was 'broke in.' "

Nothing could be done about the weather, however, and cowboys on the open prairie soon learned to respect the power of lightning in particular. George Brock of Lockhart, Texas, said that when he first saw lightning strike the ground and set the grass on fire, he jerked loose his spurs, six-shooter and pocket knife, laid them down, and ran away. To wear anything metal was considered fatal in a lightning storm.

A sudden clap of thunder at night was almost certain to start the herd moving in a frantic mass. If the drivers lost control of the frightened cattle during a storm, the herd quickly became a monstrous, irresistible force plunging through the darkness. Sometimes the friction of the speeding cattle caused weird blue flashes to quiver at the tips of their long horns.

In a stampede, it was every man for himself. "It is beef against horseflesh," a trail-driving veteran once said, "with the odds on beef for the first hundred yards."

The cowboys in their bedrolls, awakened by the cries of the night herders or by the thundering cattle, quickly mounted their horses and rode toward the head of the stampede to help break the flight. Sometimes this could be done by turning the leaders, by firing revolvers and forcing the cattle into a great milling circle.

It was a rare stampede that left no fatalities. A horse's hoof in a prairie dog hole, a slip on muddy earth, a miscalculation of distance in blinding rain or darkness—could mean instant death.

Next morning the cook would remove the spade from beneath the chuckwagon and dig a grave; the trail boss would take the Bible from his saddlebag and read services for the dead.

Teddy Blue has told what is probably the best vernacular account of such an event: "And that night it come up an awful storm. It took all four of us to hold the cattle and we didn't hold them, and when morning come there was one man missing. We went back to look for him, and we found him among the prairie dog holes, beside his horse. The horse's ribs was scraped bare of hide, and all the rest of horse and man was mashed into the ground as flat as a pancake. The only thing you could recognize was the handle of his six-shooter. We tried to think the lightning hit him, and that was what we wrote his folks down in Henrietta, Texas. But we couldn't really believe it ourselves. I'm afraid it wasn't the lightning. I'm afraid his horse stepped into one of them holes and they both went down before the stampede.

"We got a shovel—I remember it had a broken handle—and we buried him nearby, on a hillside covered with round, smooth rocks that we called niggerheads. We dug a little of the ground away underneath him and slipped his saddle blanket under him and piled niggerheads on top. That was the best we could do. The ground was hard and we didn't have no proper tools."

Finally after three months of mud, dust, rain, rivers, Indians, rustlers, short rations, and stampedes—most of the men and cattle and horses still endured. And when the cowboys heard the whistle of a train on the railroad, or saw the first sprawling false fronts of the trail town buildings, they broke into rebel yells.

It was the end of the drive, at last.

41

RANGE BOSS (above)

The success of the roundup or a trail drive rested largely upon the shoulders of the range boss or trail boss. During a roundup or a drive, the authority of the boss was as ironclad as that of a ship's captain. But to keep his job he had to know how to manage three of the most unpredictable members of the animal kingdom—cattle, horses, and men.

GATHERING CATTLE, 19TH CENTURY (on facing page, top)

In the early years of trail driving, gathering cattle was more like a hunt than a cattle roundup. The wild Longhorns hid out in the brush and chaparral, and had to be pulled out by force, or lured out with tame cattle decoys.

ROUND-UP, 20TH CENTURY (on facing page)

As trail driving developed into a major activity in the southwest, the work of rounding up cattle and getting them to market gradually became routinized. Range cattle became accustomed to seeing mounted cowboys, and an outfit of good riders on fast cow ponies could gather a herd in relatively smooth fashion.

END OF A DAY'S GATHER

At the beginning of a "gather," the roundup boss would send his men out in several directions. As soon as each rider reached a specified point, he turned back and herded all the cattle within his area back into the camp center.

THE CHUCKWAGON WAS HOME

On range or drive, the chuckwagon was home. A good cook was not only proficient at the culinary arts; he also was a combination housekeeper, morale-builder, and expert wagon driver or "bull whacker."

The cowhands usually referred to the cook as the "Old Lady," but they were careful not to offend him. He had too many subtle ways of evening the score. The cook was the aristocrat of the trail drive, a man who prized his dignity, was seldom a good rider, and had slight use for the temperamental cattle.

SINGING IN A COW CAMP

After supper in a cow camp, while the cook was washing the pots and pans, the cowboys liked to gather for some singing. If they were lucky, a fiddler would be among them. They sang rollicking songs, sad songs, unprintably ribald songs, but usually ended with a sacred hymn.

CUTTING OUT (*on facing page, top*)

When a herd had been collected, the second operation of the roundup began. Mature animals which were to be driven north to market and calves which were to be branded for return to the range, had to be separated from the herd. "Cutting out," it was called, and it was and still is the highest art of the cowboy.

ROPING (*on facing page*)

Once a steer or a calf was cut out from the herd, it had to be roped. This the rider did with his right hand, while directing his pony with the left, spinning out an oval-shaped noose over his head, and making the throw, sometimes for the animal's head, sometimes for its legs.

H.C.

R. H. Chisholm

Ezekiel Williams

Recorder

"THE OLD COW CHARGED WITH HER HEAD 'WAY DOWN, A'ROLLIN' HER EYES AND A-PAWIN' THE GROUND."

As they were cut out and roped, one by one the unbranded animals were herded or dragged over to the bonfire where the branding irons were being heated to an orange red.

FIRST BRAND RECORDED IN TEXAS

The heraldry of the range is as old as Spanish-Mexican cattle ranching. Here is shown one of the first recorded Texas brands, that of Richard H. Chisholm of Gonzales, entered before the Alamo, in 1832.

SAMUEL MAVERICK

During the Mexican War, many cattle reached maturity without being branded. Colonel Samuel A. Maverick owned such a herd near San Antonio. They went unbranded for so long that when one would stray into another rancher's territory, it was usually referred to as "One of Maverick's," or "That's a Maverick." So was created a new word in the American language.

PAGE FROM A TEXAS BRAND BOOK

Public registration of legitimate brands was established so that cattlemen could detect a blotched or illegal brand. In Texas, brands were recorded by counties; other States had State brand books.

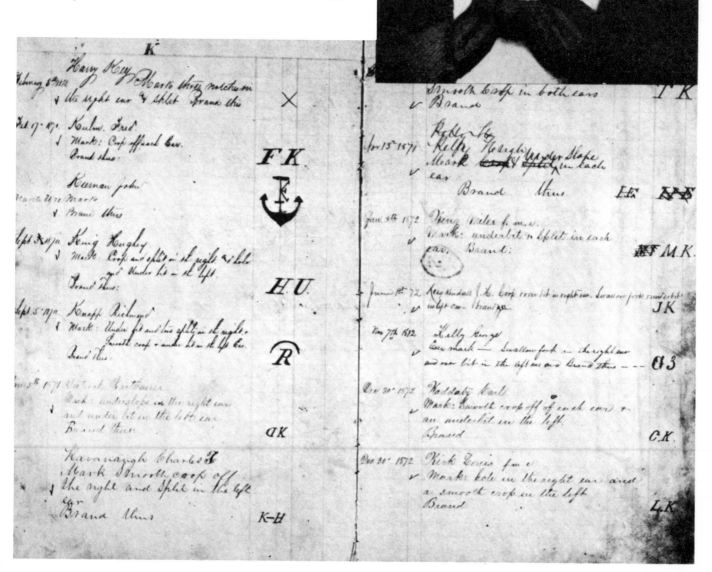

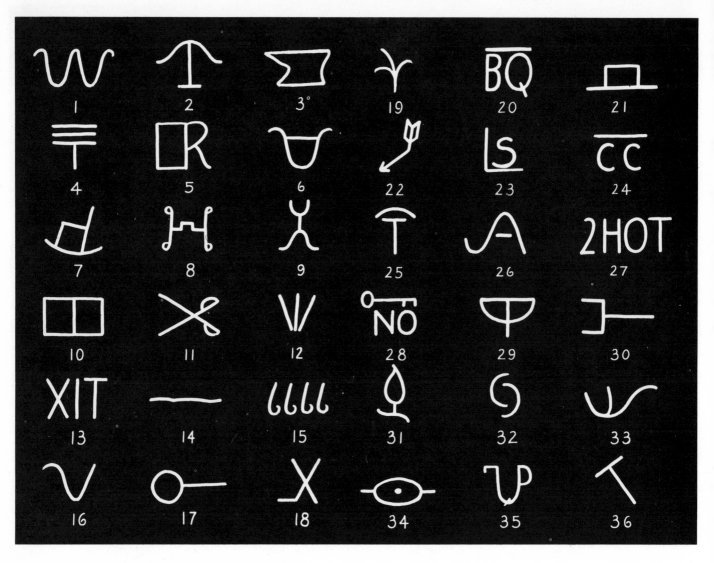

BRANDS OF THE SOUTHWEST

Some of the great brands of southwestern cattle ranching are shown above:

1. Richard King's Running W
2. Hash Knife
3. Anvil
4. Curry Comb
5. John Blocker's Block R
6. Stirrup
7. Rocking Chair
8. Spanish Bit
9. Andiron
10. Bible
11. Scissors
12. Hansford's Turkey Track
13. XIT
14. John Chisum's Long Rail
15. Burk Burnett's Four Sixes
16. Matador's Flying V
17. Glidden and Sanborn's Frying Pan
18. LX

19. Three Feathers
20. Barbeque
21. Hat
22. Broken Arrow
23. LS
24. Henry Creswell's Bar CC
25. Bugbee's Quarter Circle T
26. Goodnight and Adair's JA
27. W. E. Jackson's Too Hot
28. Cabler and Mathis' Keno
29. Captain John Rabb's Bow and Arrow
30. Driscoll's Wrench
31. Mifflin Kenedy's Laurel Leaf
32. Halff's Quien Sabe
33. Pipe
34. Hog Eye
35. Seven Up
36. Tumbling T

BRANDING, 19TH CENTURY

The operation of getting a branding iron on a stubborn cow or calf. whether in the open or in a corral, was a plain hard-muscle job.

A technique was early developed whereby two men known as flankers tackled from opposite sides. One doubled up the animal's front leg and put his knee on its head. The other flanker braced one of his feet against the animal's hind leg, stretching the other to full length. The brander then pressed the hot iron home, and the checker entered another mark in the round-up tally book.

BRANDING, 20TH CENTURY

Branding is still the toughest and roughest job on a cattle ranch. The animal is bawling and kicking, dust is flying, and over everything is the acrid smell of burned hair and hide.

TEXAS MUSTANGS (below)

In preparation for a trail drive, Texas cattlemen had to acquire a plentitude of horses. Wild horse herds were the usual source, and they were rounded up much like the wild Longhorns.

BREAKING A WILD HORSE

Wild horses not only had to be corralled and branded, they had to be broken to the saddle and bridle. The process was sometimes rough on both horses and men. In the early years of the range, quirts and spurs were freely used.

"THERE NEVER WAS A HORSE THAT COULDN'T BE RODE,

THERE NEVER WAS A RIDER THAT COULDN'T BE THROWED."

Even after a good breaking in, some high-spirited horses just naturally didn't like saddles or bridles. A back fall or roll was one method they used to shake off riders.

But a good cowman did not mind spirit in his mount. He knew a lively actor made the best cow pony and could be gentled with the right sort of training.

REMUDA

The horse herd accompanying a trail drive was known as the remuda (pronounced *remoother* in Texas). From a hundred to a hundred and fifty horses formed the average drive's remuda, and they were handled by a young waddy known as the horse wrangler. When the cattle were halted, a single rope corral was sufficient to hold a herd of trained range horses in place.

"HIS HAT WAS THROWED BACK AND HIS SPURS WAS A'JINGLIN'"

Because every item of a cowboy's costume was designed originally for utility, it has remained basically the same for almost a century.

EARLY MORNING (*on facing page, top*)

The cowboy's life revolved around the chuckwagon. In this scene the cook is just awakening, and in a few minutes will be shaking the dew from the canvas covering of his kitchen on wheels. A little later, the sleeping cowboys will start their day with the sound of his voice in all its early morning raucousness: "Arise and shine!"

"IT'S BACON AND BEANS MOST EVERY DAY.
I'D AS SOON BE EATIN' PRAIRIE HAY" (*on facing page*)

Eating was important, although food on the trail seldom varied. Black coffee, sour-dough biscuit, beans, meat and gravy. A delicacy was fresh onions, which they could find growing wild as they drove across the Indian Territory into Kansas in late spring.

READY FOR THE LONG DRIVE

Getting the average trail herd of three thousand cattle underway was as complicated an operation as starting an army on a march across country. The personnel consisted of sixteen to eighteen cowboys, a cook and his wagon, and a horse wrangler for the remuda.

HERD ON THE TRAIL (on facing page, top)

A herd on the trail moved like a sinuous snake, the lead steer and the best physical specimens "on the point." Two riders rode the point, with swing riders behind them to keep the flanks of the herd from spreading too wide.

DRAG RIDERS (on facing page)

The tail or drag riders brought up the rear, the least desirable position on a drive. The drag riders had to keep the lame and weak cattle moving, and all day they rode in clouds of dust, assailed by the heat and smells of the herd. Beginning cowboys usually received this assignment, and as they achieved experience and seniority, moved up toward the point.

NIGHT HERDERS

Each evening the herd had to be bedded down, and the night watch assigned, the men usually working in shifts of two to four hours. To keep the restive cattle quiet, the riders rode slowly around the herd, crooning to the animals. The cowboys soon learned that cattle liked slow mournful songs, the sadder the better, which may account for the dolorous quality of so many cowboy ballads.

STAMPEDE (*on facing page, top*)

That most dreaded occurrence of a trail drive—a stampede—usually originated at night. Any sudden noise, the rattle of a cook's skillet or a clap of thunder, would start the herd moving in a sudden frantic mass.

"IN A NARROW GRAVE JUST SIX BY THREE THEY LAID HIM THERE ON THE LONE PRAIRIE." (*on facing page*)

It was a rare stampede that left no fatalities. A horse's hoof in a prairie dog hole, a slip on muddy earth, a miscalculation of distance in blinding rain or darkness—could mean instant death.

Next morning the cook would remove the spade from beneath the chuckwagon and dig a grave; the trail boss would take the Bible from his saddlebag and read services for the dead.

END OF THE TRAIL DRIVE

> "I've finished the drive and drawn my money,
>   Goin' into town to see my honey."

Finally after three months of mud, dust, rain, rivers, Indians, rustlers, short rations, and stampedes—most of the men and cattle and horses still endured. When the cowboys heard the first whistle of a train on the railroad, or saw the sprawling false-fronts of the distant trail town buildings, they broke into rebel yells.

CHAPTER THREE

Rip-Roaring Trail Towns

When they reached a trail town at the end of a drive, the cowboys sometimes drove the herd right through the streets. As soon as the cattle were bedded down, all except a few herd riders were free to go into town. It was customary to pay off the men as soon as the drive ended, and with money jingling in their pockets, the cowboys were ripping and raring and ready to go. After three hard months on the trail, no one could blame them for cutting loose and raising hell.

No cowboy entering a trail town ever permitted his horse to walk or trot; all horses went in at a lope or a gallop. Pistols were fired off, but they were usually pointed skyward. With their horses' hoofs pounding the streets, their bridle chains rattling, and their voices whooping out rebel yells, they made plenty of noise. But unless they were frustrated by some undiplomatic town marshal, their spontaneous hurrahing did not last much longer or create any more havoc than a modern demonstration by college boys celebrating a football victory.

The usual first action of a trail's end cowboy was to get a haircut and have his mustache or beard properly shaped and blacked. Then he visited a clothing store for a new outfit. Emerging with new clothes, the hat and boots embellished with Texas stars, he was ready for fun and frolic.

"I remember it like it was yesterday," says Teddy Blue. "I had a new white Stetson hat that I paid ten dollars for and new pants that cost twelve dollars, and a good shirt and fancy boots. They had colored tops, red and blue, with a half-moon and star on them. Lord, I was proud of those clothes! They were the kind of clothes top hands wore, and I thought I was dressed right for the first time in my life."

After drinking some of the strong whisky which was brought into the town in carloads, and bucking the tiger with the faro dealers, the men were ready for a hoe-dig with the Calico Queens of the honkytonks.

"The cowboy," said Joseph McCoy, "enters the dance with a peculiar zest, not stopping to divest himself of his sombrero, spurs, or pistols. . . . A more odd, not to say comical, sight is not often seen than the dancing cowboy. With the front of his sombrero lifted at an angle of fully forty-five degrees, his huge spurs jingling at every step or motion, his revolvers flapping up and down like a retreating sheep's tail, his eyes lit up with excitement, liquor, and lust, he plunges in and 'hoes it down' at a terrible rate in the most approved yet awkward country style, often swinging his partner clear off of the floor for an entire circle, then 'balance all,' with an occasional demoniacal yell near akin to the war whoop of the savage Indian. All this he does, entirely oblivious to the whole world and to the balance of mankind. After dancing furiously, the entire 'set' is called to 'waltz to the bar,' where the boy is required to treat his partner and, of course, himself also; which he does not hesitate to do time and again, although it costs him fifty cents each time."

Most cowboys trailing to Kansas cow towns were from Texas, but even those from other sections were called "Texans." A Kansas traveler of the day described them as follows: "In appearance a species of centaur, half horse, half man, with immense rattling spurs, tanned skin, and dare-devil, almost ferocious faces."

A *New York Tribune* correspondent observed: "And here are . . . the identical chaps I first saw at Fair Oaks and last saw at Gettysburg. Every man of them unquestionably was in the Rebel army. Some of them have not yet worn out all of their distinctive gray clothing—keen-looking men, full of reserved force, shaggy with hair, undoubtedly terrible in a fight, yet peaceably great at cattle-driving and not demonstrative in their style of wearing six-shooters."

James Butler (Wild Bill) Hickok, who had fought against these men as a scout and spy in Missouri and Arkansas, understood them well, and shortly after he became Abilene's marshal in 1871, Hickok announced that the cowboys could wear their revolvers wherever and whenever they pleased. This was a welcome change from the rules established by the late Bear River Tom Smith.

A tall graceful man and a spectacular gun fighter, Wild Bill patrolled Texas Street by walking in the center. His long auburn hair hanging in ringlets over his shoulders and his small, finely formed hands and feet gave him a feminine appearance. But everyone respected Wild Bill as a quick-draw artist. He usually wore a pair of ivory-hilted and silver-mounted pistols thrust into a richly embroidered sash. His shirts were of the finest linen and his boots of the thinnest kid leather.

As Wild Bill's salary was rather small, he augmented his earnings by frequent gambling. He was popular with most of the cowboys.

Some other Abilene citizens were as colorful as Wild Bill. Josiah Jones was a fat and jolly saloonkeeper who kept a colony of prairie dogs for fun. When eastern visitors began offering him five dollars per pair for the prairie dogs, Jones's hobby became such a business that he complained he had no time for running his saloon. He engaged small boys to sell the animals to travelers on the Kansas Pacific.

Lou Gore and her husband, J. W. Gore, operated McCoy's Drover's Cottage, the elite hotel of one hundred rooms, with an adjoining barn spacious enough to house fifty

64

carriages and one hundred horses. Texans relished the Cottage's iced drinks, made possible by stored ice cut from the Republican River during previous winters.

McCoy had found the Gores at the St. Nicholas Hotel in St. Louis, where J. W. Gore was working as a steward. Lou was a natural-born hotel keeper, a friend to all cowmen, rich or poor, sick or well. The most hardened horse thief would have considered it a disgrace to beat a board bill at Lou Gore's Cottage.

In 1871 a pair of gambling men, Ben Thompson and Phil Coe, came to Abilene and established the Bull's Head Tavern & Gambling Saloon. For an advertisement, a huge and lascivious bull was painted on the outside wall. After some of the more prudish citizens objected to the painting, Wild Bill Hickok ordered the bull removed. Thompson ignored the order. To settle the argument peaceably, Wild Bill obtained a bucket of paint and "materially altered the offending bovine."

When John Wesley Hardin arrived in Abilene in 1871, his reputation had already preceded him. Wild Bill had in his possession a handbill sent up from Texas offering a reward for the arrest of this eighteen-year-old boy who packed a loose six-shooter. Ben Thompson of the Bull's Head Tavern had also heard of the gun prowess of this smiling young Texan with the light blue eyes.

Thompson tried to prejudice Hardin against Hickok. "He's a damyankee," said Thompson. "Picks on rebels, especially Texans, to kill."

"If Wild Bill needs killin'," replied John Wesley Hardin, "why don't you kill him yourself?"

Later Hickok and Hardin did have trouble, but no shots were fired. Wild Bill began referring to Hardin as "Little Arkansaw" and they became friendly. Hickok is said to have told Hardin he would not arrest him for any crimes he had committed in Texas, but that if he killed anyone in Abilene he would not get out of town alive.

One night Hardin was in his bed in the American Hotel when a man unlocked the door and slipped into the room. Hardin fired at the intruder and killed him. As Wild Bill drove up to the hotel in a hack to investigate the gunfire, the young Texan slipped out on the roof in such a hurry he left his trousers behind. Wild Bill ran into the hotel, and Hardin jumped down into the hack and drove away. He stole the first saddled pony he saw, and rode off toward Texas minus his trousers. Several miles below Abilene, John Wesley Hardin took a pair of pants from a luckless cowboy at gun's point, ordering the man on into town in his underdrawers. "Give Wild Bill my love," was Hardin's parting message.

Abilene's saloons bore colorful names, such as Applejack, Old Fruit, and The Pearl. Obviously christened to appeal to Texans was the Alamo, the most resplendent of the drinking houses. The Alamo boasted three sets of double-glass doors, and a bar with carefully polished brass fixtures and rails. All along the walls were huge paintings, nudes done in imitation of the Italian Renaissance painters. Music was furnished the customers continuously from pianos, raucous horns, and bull fiddles.

Wild Bill selected the Alamo as his headquarters. In 1871 a correspondent from the *Daily Kansas State Record* described a scene inside the saloon: "A bartender, with a countenance like a youthful divinity student, fabricates wonderful drinks, while the music of a piano and a violin from a raised recess, enlivens the scene, and 'soothes the savage breasts' of those who retire torn and lacerated from an unfortunate combat with the 'tiger'."

When trail towns became subject to too much law and order, suburbs developed immediately outside the legal limits. Abilene's unsavory sin den was called by several names —Texas Town, The Beer Garden, Fisher's Addition, and The Devil's Addition.

It was booming during the 1871 season. "Beer gardens, dance halls, and dancing platforms and saloons galore were there," wrote Theophilus Little, a lumberman of Abilene. "It was called 'The Devil's Addition' to Abilene, rightly named, for Hell reigned there— Supreme. Hacks were run day and night to this addition. Money and whisky flowed like water down hill, and youth and beauty and womanhood and manhood were wrecked and damned in that Valley of Perdition."

One of the more violent episodes of Abilene's lush period developed around a fair damsel of the dance halls. Her name was Jessie Hazel, admired by Phil Coe of the Bull's Head Tavern. Wild Bill Hickok was a rival for the favors of Jessie Hazel, and the two men became bitter enemies.

When Hickok accused Phil Coe of cheating at cards, the inevitable gun battle followed. Coe was killed. During the confusion, Wild Bill also accidentally killed one of his deputies, Mike Williams. In bloody anger, Wild Bill chased all the cowboys out of town and began patrolling Texas Street with a sawed-off shotgun loaded with buckshot.

1871 was Abilene's last big season. During its five-year reign as king of the cowtowns, small farmers—or nesters as the cowmen called them—had been pushing steadily westward along the Kansas Pacific until most of the free range was gone.

Cattlemen were considered natural enemies, and in February, 1872, they were ordered to stay away from Abilene:

> We, the undersigned, members of the Farmers' Protective Association, and officers and citizens of Dickinson County, Kansas, most respectfully request all who have contemplated driving Texas cattle to Abilene the coming season to seek some other point for shipment, as the inhabitants of Dickinson will no longer submit to the evils of the trade.

The big boom collapsed immediately. Before the end of 1872, the town's leaders were begging the drivers and shippers to come back, but it was too late. New boom towns were already in the making.

Another westward moving railroad, the Atchison, Topeka & Santa Fe, was preparing to share in the cattle trade. By the spring of 1871, the Santa Fe had reached Newton, sixty-five miles to the south of Abilene.

"The firing of guns in and around the town," said Cal Johnson of Newton, "was so continuous it reminded me of a Fourth of July celebration from daylight to midnight. There was shooting when I got up and when I went to bed."

And Newton's glory was as flashing and brief as a Fourth of July skyrocket. Twenty buildings went up the first month of the town's existence. They were the usual false-front structures, and some bore the names of their predecessors in Abilene.

Joseph McCoy soon arrived to establish his second stockyard, this one large enough to hold four thousand cattle. McCoy knew from experience that booming cowtowns developed rapidly, and he built his Newton yards a mile and a half from the original business section.

Grass still covered the streets of Newton when the first herds arrived. Prairie dog colonies were on every side, and wild animals were so numerous that the city council passed an ordinance prohibiting the running at large of buffaloes and other animals.

One of the few women ever to experience a trail drive was Amanda Burks, who accompanied her husband, W. F. Burks, from Nueces County, Texas, to Newton in 1871. Amanda Burks drove a buggy most of the way, experiencing lightning and hail storms, witnessing fights with rustlers and Indians, a prairie fire, and a stampede.

Cattle prices had dropped before the Burkses reached Newton, and they wintered their herd on Smoky River, a considerable distance north of the town. After selling their cattle in the spring, they made the return journey by rail to St. Louis and New Orleans, and then by water to Corpus Christi. In later years, this rail and water route was frequently used by wives of coastal cattlemen, who arranged their journeys so as to meet their trail-driving husbands in Kansas.

Gunfire was frequent in Newton, as Cal Johnson truthfully reported, but there was little bloodshed until late in the 1872 season, when a big shoot-out exploded in Perry Tuttle's dance house. Instead of a Devil's Addition, Newton had its "Hide Park," a shambling collection of dance halls and saloons south of the railroad tracks. Perry Tuttle's establishment in Hide Park was a popular rendezvous for trail drivers.

One night Mike McCluskie, the Newton marshal, was seated at a gambling table in one corner of Perry Tuttle's place when a Texas trail driver named Hugh Anderson came in on the prod. McCluskie had killed a Texan a few days earlier, and the man had been a good friend of Anderson.

Suddenly Anderson strode across the floor toward the marshal. "You're a cowardly son of a bitch!" he shouted at McCluskie. "I'm going to blow the top of your head off." Gunfire followed immediately, friends of both men joining in the shooting.

Within a few seconds, nine men lay dead or wounded on the floor. Marshal Mike McCluskie was among the dead. In Newton, the affair was always referred to as the "General Massacre."

McCluskie's successors were kept busy by Cherokee Dan Hicks, a buffalo hunter, who enjoyed getting drunk and shooting up the town. Cherokee Dan seemed to have a preference for pictorial targets. One day he was standing in front of the Bull's Head Tavern, peppering lead into the picture of a bull on that establishment's fancy signboard. When Marshal Charlie Baumann tried to stop him, Cherokee Dan shot the lawman's right thumb off and wounded him in the thigh. On a later occasion, the buffalo hunter walked into Harry Lovett's saloon and suddenly started shooting at the gaudy nude paintings which lined the walls. Harry Lovett was not a man who would stand idly by while his cherished art works were being destroyed; he opened fire with his six-shooter, and that was the end of Cherokee Dan Hicks.

For a one-season cowtown, Newton spread as much mustard as any of its longer-lived rivals.

Meanwhile the Kansas Pacific Railroad had pushed westward to Ellsworth, a town which boasted simultaneously of its iniquity and of its superior cattle shipping facilities.

Ellsworth lay flat on the treeless banks of Smoky Hill River in the midst of an endless prairie of grama grass. Its Main Street, three blocks of frame structures, ran parallel with the railroad tracks.

From Abilene, Lou and J. W. Gore brought their respectable Drover's Cottage. Parts of this building and some of the saloons were loaded on railroad cars and shipped in sections from Abilene to Ellsworth. The term "hell on wheels" is said to have originated from this rail movement of honkytonks and gambling hells from one trail town to another. The American House, Beebe's General Store, and Brennan's Saloon were other famed landmarks in the town.

Ellsworth began operating as a cattle-shipping point in 1871, but only a few herds were received in the yards that season. The following year the number increased, several herds coming in after the drivers discovered Abilene was a closed market.

The Kansas Pacific, sensing an alert rival for the cattle trade in the new Santa Fe Railroad, gave considerable financial support to the development of Ellsworth. Under the railroad's direction a new cattle trail was surveyed from Ellsworth southeast to the old Chisholm Trail, joining it between the Salt Fork of the Arkansas and Pond Creek. It was called the Ellsworth Cattle Trail. To advertise the new trail and Ellsworth's advantages, the Kansas Pacific published a *Guide Map of the Great Texas Cattle Trail From Red River Crossing to the Old Reliable Kansas Pacific Railway*. Copies were distributed throughout the ranching country.

The new trail and the advertising paid off in 1873. By the end of May more than 100,000 Longhorns had reached the Ellsworth area. Two weeks later, 50,000 more had arrived. It looked like a big season for the cattlemen, but when the financial panic of 1873 struck Kansas in late summer, the cattle market collapsed so suddenly several drivers and shippers were immediately bankrupt.

In the meantime Ellsworth had become a roaring trail town, with the frozen market adding to the supercharged atmosphere. Every night hundreds of idle cowboys ripped through the streets and "hurrahed" the saloons. In June a jail was completed, and the Ellsworth *Reporter* described it as the most comfortable place in town, but warned its readers that too many should not crowd into the building at once.

Ben Thompson, who had lost his partner Phil Coe in Abilene, joined forces in Ellsworth with his brother, Bully Bill Thompson. The Thompsons were English-born and had served in the Confederate army, fighting to the end of the war when they rode with Joe Shelby on his venture into Mexico. The brothers operated a gambling concession and saloon in Arthur Larkin's Grand Central Hotel. To meet competition from the more refined Drover's Cottage, the Thompsons induced Larkin to construct in front of the hostelry the only limestone rock sidewalk west of Kansas City. It was twelve feet wide, was covered with wooden awnings, and was complete with a bench for sidewalk loafers.

The darlings of Ellsworth's dance halls dressed as well as their modish sisters in the east, wearing the latest style of headgear derived from hats of western buffalo hunters. Keeping up to date with *Godey's Lady's Book* may have seemed too sedate for a certain lady called Prairie Rose. One night she bet a cowboy fifty dollars she would walk unclothed down the main street of Ellsworth. This she did next morning at five o'clock, a six-gun in each hand, threatening to shoot out any eye that showed. The cowboys must have respected Prairie Rose's marksmanship. At any rate, no shots were fired.

With the assistance of the Texas cowboys, Ben and Bill Thompson "treed" Ellsworth, and for a time practically ran the town to suit themselves. Finally a sheriff, a marshal and four deputies restored law and order. But one hot August afternoon the Thompson brothers both got drunk and began making trouble for the deputy marshals, whose nicknames were Brocky Jack, Happy Jack, Long Jack and High Low Jack. In the midst of the fracas, Sheriff Chauncey Whitney appeared and was shot and killed by Bill Thompson.

As the Thompsons were Texans, a small army of trail drivers gathered to protect them. Bill was assisted out of town on a fast horse, while Ben remained in the Grand Central Hotel, armed with a double-barreled shotgun. When the deputy marshals all refused to try to arrest Ben Thompson, the mayor discharged them and arranged a deal with the gambler. Ben agreed to be charged with shooting at Happy Jack, but when Happy Jack declined to press the charge, the case was dismissed.

Meanwhile a posse of indignant citizens had gone in pursuit of Bill Thompson. As the citizens dashed out of town, another Texas gambler, Cad Pierce, offered a thousand dollars for the capture of the posse. The posse did not find Bill, and nobody chased the posse for Cad Pierce's reward money.

Not long afterward, Ben Thompson quietly left town, but his friend Cad Pierce remained too long and was killed in a street duel with a new deputy, Ed Crawford.

Lawless or not, visitors poured into the town. Some amateur actors of the Sixth Cavalry came over from Fort Harker and staged a boisterous drama for the guests of the Drover's Cottage. And one anonymous visitor wrote a piece for the Ellsworth *Reporter:*

"This little border town of Ellsworth is not the most moral one in the world. During the cattle season, which, I am told, only lasts during the summer and fall, it presents a scene seldom witnessed in any other section. Here you see in the streets . . . the tall, long-haired Texas herder, with his heavy jingling spurs and pairs of six-shooters . . . the keen stock buyers; the wealthy Texas drovers; dead beats; 'cappers'; pick-pockets; horse thieves; a cavalry of Texas ponies; and scores of *demimonde.*

"Gambling of every description is carried on without any attempt at privacy. I am told that there are some 75 professional gamblers in town, and every day we hear of some of their sharp tricks. Whisky-selling seems to be the most profitable business. But there are many honorable business men here, who are doing a heavy business."

The temporary collapse of the cattle trade in 1873, however, had marked the end of Ellsworth as the principal trail town. About half of the large herds driven in during the summer had to be winter-quartered in Kansas, or moved to Colorado. Other thousands of cattle were slaughtered for tallow, or were sold at a loss to Indian agencies.

Once again it was the Santa Fe Railroad's turn to share in the cattle trade. A branch had pushed south from Newton to Wichita, and during the 1873 season Ellsworth's chief rival was this new boomtown on the Arkansas River.

Having seen other trail towns turn conservative and drive the impetuous cowmen and their cattle away, Wichita's backers attempted to convince all comers that the new shipping center would be different. Signs were posted on the trails and outside the town: EVERYTHING GOES IN WICHITA.

By 1874, Wichita was the leading shipping center, with two hundred thousand cattle and two thousand cowboys swarming into the area at the height of the season. Ben Thompson came down from Ellsworth and set up his gambling tables at the Keno House. Thompson and the cowboys were soon running Wichita to suit themselves. "Shootin' irons" became the law.

Wichita settlers finally decided they needed some real law and order. One of the men they employed to keep the peace was Deputy Marshal Wyatt Earp. Wyatt Earp had been a stagecoach driver in Arizona, a prizefight referee in Wyoming railroad camps, and a buffalo hunter in Kansas. He had been in Ellsworth briefly, refusing an offer to become marshal there in 1873. But one day on May, 1874, he got mixed up in a free-for-all fist fight in Wichita and was arrested. A few minutes after his arrest, a bunch of cowboys started hurrahing the town, and Wyatt Earp offered to help the deputy marshal quiet them down. After the affair was over, the mayor of Wichita offered Wyatt Earp a job as deputy marshal.

"I'll take it," said Earp, and in Wichita he began a career that would lead him into many a frontier town of the developing West.

One of Wyatt Earp's friends caused the deputy marshal considerable trouble. His name was Abel "Shanghai" Pierce, a jovial full-bearded giant whose voice could be heard half a mile. He was six feet, four inches tall, and weighed two hundred and twenty pounds. He was one of the first ranchers to send stock up the overland trails, and by 1874 was a leading cattle buyer.

So many legends have been woven around Shanghai Pierce that it is difficult to separate fact from fiction. His nickname is said to have originated one day when he put on a pair of oversized spurs. "Great Day!" he shouted. "Them things make me look just like an old Shanghai rooster!" Pierce's ranch was in the Texas coastland ranching country on Matagorda Bay, and his herds of Matagorda steers were known in all the Kansas trail towns as "Shanghai Pierce's sea lions."

He was proud of those rangy mossyhorns. "They're my sea lions!" he would roar. "They come right out of the Gulf of Mexico!"

In Wichita one evening, Pierce was raising merry hell in Billy Collins' saloon. Earp took away his gun, and told him to get out of town until he was sober. Pierce's reply was that he never took a drink but he obeyed the order. Afterwards, twenty of Pierce's cowboys rode into town, gunning for Wyatt. The deputy marshal arrested them, disarmed them, and fined each one of them a hundred dollars. Blithely carrying the first walking cane ever seen in Kansas, Shanghai came back into Wichita, and cheerfully paid the two thousand dollars in fines.

Some years later when Shanghai Pierce became wealthy, he spent $10,000 for a 20-foot bronze statue of himself, and had it set up on his Rancho Grande on the Tres Palacios. Before he would accept the statue, he called in an old Negro employee, Jesse Duncan. "Is it all right, Jesse?" asked Pierce. "That thing look like me?"

70

"Yessir," said Duncan, with a suppressed grin, "it's you, all right, Mister Shanghai."

The statue now stands guard over Pierce's grave near Blessing, Texas, a town which he named. For years Pierce had been trying to persuade the railroad to build a station adjoining his ranch. When the railroad finally started constructing the station, Shanghai ordered the workmen to paint the words THANK GOD on its sides. The railroad company prevailed upon him to substitute the word BLESSING for THANK GOD.

A much more important memorial left by Shanghai Pierce is a breed of cattle, the American Brahman. On a tour through the Orient, Pierce conceived the idea of introducing Brahman cattle to the Texas coastlands as a means of combating the prevalent tick fever. Returning home, he bought two Brahmans from a circus, and proved his theory that ticks would not affect them. Although Pierce died before he could import Brahmans from India, his nephew A. P. Borden did so, and conducted the first breeding experiments on the Rancho Grande that led to the development of the present-day American Brahmans.

George Peshaur, a gun-toting pal of Ben Thompson, disapproved of the manner in which Wyatt Earp was taming Wichita. When Peshaur tried to use a young cowboy as a gunman against the marshal, Earp turned on Peshaur and whipped him to a finish in a fist fight, blacking both his eyes and smashing his nose.

One of Peshaur's friends was Mannen Clements, a Texas trail boss. Clements said it was not a fair fight, and with his brothers—Joe, Jim, and Gip—rode into Wichita early one morning in 1874, aiming to "tree" the town and have some fun with Wyatt Earp.

The deputy marshal met the Clements brothers on the Cowskin Creek bridge. "Mannen, put up your gun and take your outfit back to camp," ordered Earp.

"You put up your gun and maybe I will," said Mannen.

Earp slid his gun into his holster. Mannen Clements and his brothers followed suit, then rode on into town. Wyatt Earp was smart enough not to press such matters with the Clements brothers, and they spent a quiet morning. By similar diplomatic actions, he finally persuaded the cowboys to check their guns in racks before they started their drinking in Wichita.

The inevitable shantytown adjunct of Wichita was known as Delano. Here Rowdy Joe Lowe and John (Red) Beard operated rival dance halls. Rowdy Joe later became a train robber and was killed while holding up a Union Pacific train near Big Springs, Nebraska.

George Custer's famed Seventh Cavalry was stationed near Wichita in 1873, and during that year there was a pitched battle in Delano between the cavalrymen and the Texans. The fight started in Red Beard's place. A cavalryman tried to move in on a girl who was dancing with a cowboy. Immediately fists began flying, and revolvers began exploding in the low-ceilinged dance hall. One soldier was killed, two others wounded, mirrors and glassware were smashed, but no Texans were hurt. Almost all of the cowboys were Confederate veterans, and they disliked the blue uniforms of the army.

Joseph McCoy, who had deserted the Kansas Pacific for the Santa Fe, built a new stockyard in Wichita. He added a sideline to his business that was indeed significant of things to come. Foreseeing the end of the open range, McCoy began selling wrought-iron fencing guaranteed not to "rot, burn, blow, or fall down."

Hays City, west of Ellsworth on the Kansas Pacific, succeeded Wichita briefly as the leading cattle shipping point. "The town," said one of its early inhabitants, "was lively but not moral." Hays City boomed so fast, some visitors had to sleep in the railroad's crew cars. Amidst the confusion, one gentleman mis-read a street sign, and later recorded his error in the Manhattan (Kansas) *Standard*.

"As we sauntered slowly up the street we noticed on a dilapidated looking building a large sign informing all beholders that 'General Outfitting' could be obtained by enquiring within. Seeing no show window, and no display of goods, and being of an inquiring turn of mind, we entered. Instead of seeing a smiling, polite salesman, anxious to show us his goods, as we expected, we were welcomed by two or three very pretty smiling young ladies. We saw no goods, except feminine. Seeing that we had got into the 'wrong pew,' and being rather bashful, in spite of the fascinating appearance of the aforesaid young ladies, we disappeared."

One of the big events of Hays' trail town period was the visit of Phineas T. Barnum who came in his fancy railroad car looking for wild men to use in his circus. When the local poker players heard of Barnum's presence, they resolved to make a sucker out of the great showman. Barnum's downfall was so crushing the Topeka *Daily Kansas State Record* reported the event in detail:

"P. T. Barnum, wishing to gratify his taste for curiosities, stopped off at Hays City to see the 'man-eaters' of that town 'eat.' " He fell in with several of the more carnal-minded youth of the place, who invited him to be sociable and take a hand at poker. The cards that were dealt to his companions literally 'knocked the spots' of anything Mr. Barnum had ever 'held' in his life, and, when the exercises of the solemn occasion were ended, Phineas mourned the departure of $150 that he will never see, not any more. 'Wooly horses' and 'Feejee mermaids' are nice things to have, but they don't weigh out much playing poker at Hays City. Barnum will probably incorporate his Hays City experience into his famous lecture, 'How to Make Money.' "

For several years, Fort Hays had dominated Hays City, which had been a depot for Santa Fe trade long before the cattle period. The fort's chaplain came to Hays every Sunday to read sermons from a freight platform, but few converts were recorded.

The Seventh Cavalry stationed at the fort had kept things lively around Wichita the previous year, and was now a source of considerable trouble for Hays City. Tom Custer, brother of the famous George, considered himself immune from arrest, and at nightfall would ride through the town shooting wildly in all directions. He delighted in riding into saloons, jumping his horse upon billiard tables, and raising hell in general. One night when his horse refused to make the table jump, Custer dismounted and shot the animal there in the billiard hall.

When Wild Bill Hickok was marshal of Hays, he once tried to tame Tom Custer. Wild Bill shot Custer's horse, arrested the officer, and fined him heavily. A short time later, Tom Custer and three soldiers jumped Hickok in a saloon. Wild Bill managed to escape by firing backwards over his shoulder at the man who was forcing him to the floor. Tom Custer retaliated by calling out most of the Seventh Cavalry as avengers, and Wild Bill was forced to leave Hays City hurriedly on an eastbound Kansas Pacific freight train.

72

"WE ALL HIT TOWN, AND WE HIT HER ON THE FLY—
WE BEDDED DOWN THE CATTLE ON A HILL NEARBY"

When they reached a trail town at the end of a drive, the cowboys sometimes drove the cattle right through the streets.

HOE-DIGGING WITH THE CALICO QUEENS (below)

After drinking some of the strong whiskey which was brought into the town in carloads, the men were ready for a hoe-dig with the calico queens of the honkytonks.

CHANGING OF THE GUARD

Some unlucky cowboys had to stay with the herd while the lucky ones made merry in town. But no matter what hour the noisy celebrators returned to camp, the relieved first-shift guards would gallop off to town to salvage what joys they could from the waning night.

TRAIL DRIVERS OF TEXAS

As most cowboys trailing to Kansas cow towns were from Texas, those from other sections were also called "Texans." A traveler of the day described them as follows: "In appearance a species of centaur, half horse, half man, with immense rattling spurs, tanned skin, and dare-devil, almost ferocious faces."

WILD BILL HICKOK

James Butler (Wild Bill) Hickok, who had fought against these men as a scout and spy in Missouri and Arkansas, understood them well, and shortly after he became Abilene's marshal in 1871, Hickok announced that the cowboys could wear their revolvers wherever and whenever they pleased. A tall graceful man and a spectacular gun fighter, Wild Bill was popular with most of the cowboys.

LOU GORE AND THE DROVER'S COTTAGE

Lou Gore and her husband, J. W. Gore, operated
McCoy's Drover's Cottage, the elite hotel of one
hundred rooms with an adjoining barn spacious
enough to house fifty carriages and one hundred
horses. Lou was a friend to all cowmen, rich or
poor, sick or well, and the most hardened horse
thief would have considered it a disgrace to beat
a board bill at Lou Gore's Cottage.

BEN THOMPSON (right) AND
JOHN WESLEY HARDIN (above)

Gambling man Ben Thompson came to
Abilene in 1871 and established the Bull's
Head Tavern. He had some arguments with
Wild Bill Hickok, and when gunman John
Wesley Hardin arrived in town, Thompson
tried to prejudice the young killer against the
marshal. "He's a damyankee," said Thomp-
son. "Picks on rebels, especially Texans."
"If Wild Bill needs killin'," replied John
Wesley, "why don't you kill him yoreself?"

PHOTOGRAPH GALLERY

Every trail town had at least one photograph gallery strategically located near a popular saloon. Visiting cowboys enjoyed having their "pictures taken." Many of the photographs in this collection were made in pine-board studios such as the one shown above.

"THE DEVIL'S ADDITION" (below)

When trail towns became subject to too much law and order, suburbs developed immediately outside the legal limits. Abilene's unsavory sin den was called by several names—Texas Town, the Beer Garden, Fisher's Addition, and the Devil's Addition.

RESULT OF A MISS DEAL

One of the more violent episodes of Abilene's lush period developed from a feud between Wild Bill Hickok and gambler Phil Coe. When Hickok accused Coe of cheating at cards, a gun battle followed. Coe and one of Hickok's deputies were killed.

SANTA FE RAILROAD NEAR NEWTON (*on facing page, top*)

By the spring of 1871, the Santa Fe railroad had reached Newton, and that year was Abilene's last big season. As Newton was sixty-five miles closer to Texas, the Santa Fe was soon taking a big share of the cattle trade from the Kansas Pacific.

ELLSWORTH, KANSAS (*on facing page*)

Newton's successor was Ellsworth, west of Abilene on the Kansas Pacific. Ellsworth was a town which boasted simultaneously of its iniquity and of its superior cattle shipping facilities.

PERMANENT SETTLERS

Nearby on the prairie were the homes of more permanent citizens, most of them log and sod houses similar to this one.

BOOM TOWN

Ellsworth was soon a roaring trail town. In 1873, the national financial panic added to the super-charged atmosphere. By early summer, over one hundred thousand cattle were bivouacked around the town, awaiting a rise in prices. Every night hundreds of idle cowboys ripped through the streets and "hurrahed" the saloons.

BULLY BILL THOMPSON

Bill Thompson and his brother Ben were operating a saloon in Ellsworth's Grand Central Hotel.

84

WICHITA WELCOMES THE SANTA FE (*above*)

Meanwhile, a branch of the Santa Fe Railroad had pushed south from Newton to Wichita, and during the 1873 season Ellsworth's chief rival was this new boomtown on the Arkansas River.

COWBOYS "HURRAHING" A TRAIL TOWN (*on facing page, top*)
With the assistance of Texas cowboys, Ben and Bill Thompson "treed" Ellsworth, and ran the town to suit themselves.

PRAIRIE ROSE WAS HERE (*on facing page*)

One night a certain dance hall girl named Prairie Rose bet a cowboy fifty dollars she would walk unclothed down the main street of Ellsworth. This she did next morning at five o'clock, a six-gun in each hand, threatening to shoot out any eye that showed. The cowboys must have respected Prairie Rose's marksmanship. At any rate, no shots were fired.

"EVERYTHING GOES IN WICHITA"

Having seen other trail towns turn conservative and drive the impetuous cowmen and their cattle away, Wichita's backers tried to convince all comers that the new shipping center would be different. Signs were posted on the trails and outside the town: EVERYTHING GOES IN WICHITA. By 1874, Wichita was the leading shipping center, with two hundred thousand cattle and two thousand cowboys swarming into the area at the height of the season.

WYATT EARP

Wyatt Earp was one of Wichita's first deputy marshals. Here he began an exciting career that would take him into many a frontier town of the developing west.

MANNEN CLEMENTS

Mannen Clements, a fighting trail boss from Texas, gave Wyatt Earp a hard time. When Clements and his brothers rode into Wichita firing off their six-guns, Earp drew his gun and ordered them to rack their weapons before starting their drinking. "You put up your gun and maybe I will," said Mannen. Earp calmly slid his gun into its holster, and the Clements brothers spent a quiet morning in Wichita.

SHANGHAI PIERCE AND STATUE

A frequent visitor to Wichita was Abel (Shanghai) Pierce, a jovial full-bearded giant whose voice could be heard half a mile. Pierce was a rancher on the Texas coastland, and always referred to his cattle as "sea lions." When he became wealthy he spent $10,000 for a huge bronze statue of himself and had it set up on his ranch. The statue now stands guard over Pierce's grave near Blessing, Texas.

ROWDY JOE LOWE

The inevitable shantytown adjunct of Wichita was known as Delano. Here Rowdy Joe Lowe and John "Red" Beard operated rival dance halls. Rowdy Joe later became a train robber and was killed while holding up a Union Pacific train near Big Springs, Nebraska.

HAYS CITY, KANSAS, AGED FOUR WEEKS

Hays City, west of Ellsworth on the Kansas Pacific, succeeded Wichita briefly as the leading cattle shipping point. "The town," said one of its earliest inhabitants, "was lively but not moral."

HOTEL ON WHEELS

Hays City boomed so fast, some visitors had to sleep in the Kansas Pacific Railroad's crew cars.

FORT HAYS (*above*) *AND HAYS CITY STAGECOACH* (*on facing page*)
For several years, Fort Hays had dominated Hays City, which had been a depot for Santa Fe trade long before the cattle period. The fort's chaplain came to Hays every Sunday to read sermons from a freight platform, but few converts were recorded.

Four sets of Soldiers. Barracks. Mess Halls. Kitchens & Wash

This view furnished by Gen Van Vliet Dec 26/73 Jos Pettijohn Ks

6057 q 23

TOM CUSTER OF THE SEVENTH CAVALRY

The Seventh Cavalry stationed at the fort was a source of considerable trouble for the town. Tom Custer, brother of the famous George, considered himself immune from arrest, and at nightfall would ride through Hays City shooting wildly in all directions. He delighted in riding into saloons, jumping his horse upon billiard tables, and raising hell in general.

CHAPTER FOUR

The Saga of Dodge City

Meanwhile an old trade of the western prairies was developing rapidly into a big business. On the western fringes of the shifting trail towns, the camps of the buffalo hunters were becoming more numerous. Small trading centers, established for the hunters, soon were mushrooming into towns.

For centuries the buffalo had served as a source of food, clothing and shelter for the plains Indians. When the white men first pushed westward, and for many years afterward, buffalo were considered unworthy of exploitation. Finally, when the fur trappers had practically exterminated the beaver and other animals, they turned to the buffalo for skins.

One of the great hunters was William F. Cody, who won his legendary name, Buffalo Bill, during this time. After the Kansas Pacific Railroad reached Hays City, the contracting firm needed a good buffalo hunter to supply meat for the railroad laborers. Cody was recommended by Wild Bill Hickok, and the contractors offered him five hundred dollars a month if he could supply enough buffalo meat to feed the hungry men. Buffalo Bill worked for the company for seventeen months, and by his own count killed four thousand, two hundred and eighty buffalo during that time. The railroad workers are said to have given Cody the name that stayed with him the remainder of his life.

Many of the famed peace officers of the trail towns also began their careers as buffalo hunters, including Wyatt Earp, Jack Bridges, Pat Garrett, and William Barclay (Bat) Masterson.

Experienced buffalo hunters knew how to fire so as to keep a herd milling, bringing a new target into place after each shot. Favorite weapons of the hunters were Springfield "needle guns" and the Sharps rifle, which were sometimes used with telescopic sights and placed on tripods because the barrels became so hot from continuous firing. Needle guns received their name from the long firing pins which plunged through paper cartridges to

93

strike the primers. Buffalo Bill used a Springfield which he called *Lucretia Borgia,* and he preferred firing from horseback. He would ride to the head of the herd and turn the leaders until he had the buffaloes revolving in a circle. Then he shot the animals which broke off in a straight line.

A good hunter could average between fifty and a hundred buffalo killed per day. Robert M. Wright, buffalo hide trader of Dodge City, said the record was 120 killed at one stand in forty minutes by Tom Nixon. "From the 18th of September to the 20th of October, he killed two thousand, one hundred and seventy-three buffaloes," the Dodge City *Times* reported on August 18, 1877.

When it was discovered that buffalo hides made excellent machine belting, demand and prices increased sharply. The railroads extending across the plains made possible economical shipments to the eastern markets, and cattlemen welcomed and assisted in the obliteration of the buffalo herds which supported the Indians and also interfered with their cattle.

The railroads had split the buffalo into two great herds. In 1870, four million buffalo roamed south of the Platte; one half million were on the northern plains. Between 1871 and 1875 practically all of the southern buffalo were slain. The slaughter not only wiped out the buffalo, it also ended the civilization of the plains Indians. But it was a boon to the cattlemen.

During the period of greatest slaughter, a bill was proposed in the Texas legislature to protect the buffalo from the hunters. General Phil Sheridan, who wanted to destroy the buffalo herds in order to subdue the Indians, appeared before the legislature to oppose the bill. He predicted that the passing of the buffalo would herald the greatest era of the cattle trade. "Your prairies can be covered with cattle, and the cowboy will follow the hunter as a second forerunner of an advanced civilization." Sheridan's prediction proved true. Even before the last of the buffalo had vanished, cattle herds began moving into the millions of acres of grassy buffalo range.

In the early days of the slaughter, buffalo skinning was considered an ignominious trade, but as wages increased skinning became more respectable. In a hunting party only one or two men used rifles, the others being skinners. Skillful skinners could "peel" a large buffalo in five minutes.

After a buffalo skin was removed, it was pegged to the ground and left in the sun to dry. In his biography, John R. Cook tells of having at one time two thousand hides stacked up and drying. "890 of them I had skinned and was so credited," he says.

On the Santa Fe Trail five miles west of Fort Dodge, a sod house was erected in 1871 to serve the buffalo hunters of that area. The place was known as Buffalo City. When the Santa Fe Railroad's construction gangs arrived in 1872, they found beside the old Santa Fe Trail a general store, three dance halls, and six saloons. On all sides were huge piles of buffalo bones, not then considered to be of value.

The town now bore the name of Dodge City, after Fort Dodge. Dodge, the old-timers called it, and they fondly hailed the place as "the cowboy capital." Dodge was also the last and longest lived of all the Kansas trail towns.

Wright & Rath were the largest shippers of buffalo hides in Dodge, sending out 200,-000 hides the first winter the Santa Fe Railroad reached Dodge City. "I think there were at least as many more shipped from there," says Robert M. Wright, "besides two hundred cars of buffalo hindquarters and two cars of buffalo tongues."

Dodge was a ready-made trail town. Two veteran buffalo hunters, Ed Jones and Joe Plummer, had hauled buffalo hides north from Texas, and their trace was soon converted into a route for cattle herds. Originally known as the Jones and Plummer Trail, it soon became the Dodge City Trail, and later the Western Trail. Before its glory was ended the great Western Trail ran all the way from Bandera, Texas, through Dodge City to Ogallala, Nebraska, and on across the Sioux reservations in the Dakotas to Calgary, Canada.

In the Texas buffalo hunting grounds where Jones and Plummer operated, another hide trading center developed around Fort Griffin. At this supply base, F. E. Conrad's general merchandise store sometimes averaged sales of $2500 daily in guns and ammunition to buffalo hunters.

"The town of Griffin," wrote a reporter for the Galveston *News,* "is supported by buffalo hunters and is their general rendezvous in this section. The number of hunters on the ranges this season is estimated at 1500. We saw at Griffin a plat of ground of about four acres covered with buffalo hides spread out to dry, besides a large quantity piled up for shipment. These hides are worth in this place from $1.00 to $1.60 each. The generally accepted idea of the exciting chase in buffalo hunting is not the plan pursued by the men who make it a regular business. They use the needle gun with telescope, buy powder by the keg, their lead in bulks and the shells, and make their own cartridges."

Early cattle drivers on the Dodge City Trail usually funneled their cattle north through Fort Griffin, seeking protection from marauding bands of Comanches. Below the hill where the fort stood was "the Flat," a small cluster of adobes and frame shacks on the Clear Fork of the Brazos.

Nearby were the Tonkawas, friendly Indians, who evidently believed the cattle herds were replacements for the buffalo killed by the white hunters. It was said that more beeves were lost to the friendly Tonkawas than to the unfriendly Comanches.

Few cattle drivers passed Fort Griffin without stopping over at the Bee Hive Saloon, which had on its front a honeysuckle-bordered sign:

> Within this hive we're all alive
> Good whiskey makes us funny,
> So if you're dry come up and try
> The flavor of our honey.

Gambling was the favorite relaxation for drivers and buffalo hunters, and faro was the popular game.

During its heyday, Fort Griffin's "Flat" boasted some remarkable characters, including the ubiquitous John "Doc" Holliday and his strong-willed inamorata, Big Nose Kate Fisher.

Doc Holliday was originally a Georgia dentist, a thin, haggard-faced man, with deep-set blue eyes and a neatly trimmed mustache. He had come west to Texas in hopes of improving his tubercular condition, opened an office in Dallas, and then turned to gambling. Wyatt Earp said that he once saw him bet ten thousand dollars on the turn of a card.

In Fort Griffin, Doc Holliday teamed up with Big Nose Kate Fisher, who in spite of her name was a rather attractive although fiery-tempered dance hall girl. One night in January, 1878, Holliday killed Ed Bailey in a fight over a poker game, and the Fort Griffin marshal, for lack of a jail, imprisoned the gambler in a hotel room. Learning that Bailey's friends were planning a lynching party for Holliday, Big Nose Kate packed their belongings in a bag, secretly obtained two fast-footed horses, and then set fire to the rear end of the hotel in which her lover was imprisoned.

As soon as everybody in Fort Griffin ran to fight the flames, Big Nose Kate went to Holliday's room, threw down on the surprised guard with her six-shooter, disarmed him, gave Holliday the gun, and then hurried him out to the waiting horses. By the time the fire was out, the redoubtable pair were miles away.

Most mysterious inhabitant of Fort Griffin was Lottie Deno, a good-looking, red-haired gambling woman. She lived in a cottage alone, and received no visitors. The cattlemen, who called her "Mystic Maude," learned to respect the lady's gambling abilities. But she remains a mystery, vanishing completely when she left Fort Griffin.

With its continual cattle traffic, Fort Griffin became a boom town. As the buffalo disappeared, many of the hunters turned to outlawry. To combat them, masked vigilantes were organized. Horse thievery was considered so heinous a crime that the vigilantes discontinued placarding the dead with their names. Instead they labeled the victims "Horse Thief No. 5," "Horse Thief No. 6," etc., and left them to swing anonymously from the trees along the Clear Fork.

From Fort Griffin the drovers headed north, striking Red River at a place which came to be known as Doan's Crossing. At this point, Judge C. F. Doan and his nephew, Corwin Doan, opened a large store, selling whiskey, guns, ammunition, saddles and blankets. It was a favorite stopping place for Texas cattlemen throughout the lifetime of the Western Trail.

The Bar X Ranch, owned by English investors, was near Doan's Crossing. One day in 1887 a company emissary, Arthur James Balfour, arrived unannounced on the mail stage. He stepped off the stage, a faultlessly dressed Britisher, and walked into Doan's Store. After purchasing a pair of duck overalls, a big hat, boots, and a red bandanna, Balfour retired to a back room and changed costumes. When he arrived at the Bar X Ranch, he asked for a job as cowhand and got it.

During the next ten days, Balfour learned why the ranch was earning no profits for his colleagues. Returning to Doan's Store, he changed back to his English gentleman's costume, summoned the manager of the ranch, fired him, and cabled information to England which saved his company a considerable fortune.

North from Doan's Crossing, the next base on the Western Trail was Camp Supply in Indian Territory. From this army center, used by George Custer during his operations against the Southern Cheyennes, the remainder of the route to Dodge was over a well-traveled wagon trail, worn deep across the rolling prairie.

One of the first cattlemen to make the long drive over this trail from Texas through Dodge City and beyond to the Sioux country was James H. Cook. In 1876, while still a young cow waddy, Cook helped drive a herd from the Nueces River deep in southeast Texas all the way to the Dakotas. It was the first great herd of cattle to be driven through western Nebraska. The cattle were to be used to supply reservation Indians.

While camped on the Niobrara River, Cook and his companions were caught in the backwash of the Custer defeat on the Little Horn. A party of Sioux warriors swarmed down on the cowboys and charged their camp, "a yelling, screeching line of riders, beautifully painted and nearly naked. Some had rifles and pistols, but the greater part were armed with bows and arrows. Most of our little band felt, I think, that our time on earth would soon be ended; but, as the Indians did not shoot, none of us pulled a gun. They were all riding bareback, and they certainly made an impressive picture. Their impetuous rush soon brought them upon us, and they formed a complete circle about us. One old warrior with a badly scarred face dashed up almost to my feet, where he pulled his horse to a sudden stop."

The warrior wanted to know what the cowboys were doing in his country. Cook, who had learned a few words of Sioux, told him that he and his companions had just driven a herd of cattle to the Indians on the Missouri River. "My Lacota (Sioux) friends have bad hearts," said Cook. "But they must not kill the cowboys who bring the cattle which the Great Father sends to them, or the soldiers will come in great numbers and with many big guns and wipe out the Sioux nation."

Immediately the Indian turned to his war party and explained what the white men were doing. "Yells of 'How! how!' came back to him from every direction. Packing our camp outfit on our ponies, we started in to round up our saddle horses and drive them across the river, the entire band of Indians helping us. Their mood had changed, and there were many 'How's!' exchanged as we parted on the south side of the Niobrara."

In addition to seeing new country and experiencing new adventures, trail drivers on the Western Trail were also handling a new breed of cattle. The scrawny Longhorns were still plentiful, but they were gradually being displaced by a crossbreed of rangy Durhams, later known as Shorthorns. Texas cattlemen were also importing Hereford bulls from Kentucky where Henry Clay had introduced them in 1817. A crossing of Herefords with Longhorns added as much as three hundred pounds to the weight of the steers, and "Whitefaces" instead of "Longhorns" would soon become the symbol of trail cattle.

Trading center and "capital city" of the trail was of course Dodge City, a fabulous town of innumerable legends for a golden decade. Its sprawling collection of false-front wooden buildings was a familiar sight to thousands of cowboys throughout the West. Its saloons and gambling dens and theaters—Beatty and Kelley's Alhambra, the Dodge Opera House, Delmonico's Restaurant, the Alamo, the Long Branch, the Comique, the Lady Gay—were known from the Rio Grande to the Canadian border.

The legendary Long Branch Saloon was owned by Chalk Beeson and Bill Harris, with Luke Short running the gambling concessions. Under its ornate chandeliers, Doc

97

Holliday once saved Wyatt Earp's life. In its entranceway, Clay Allison and Earp threw down on each other to begin a bloodless feud. And over one of its gaming tables, a celebrated faro dealer, Cockeyed Frank Loving, killed a gambler in a quick gunfight.

It was in the Long Branch that Luke Short employed the first female pianist to perform in a Dodge saloon. Naturally she drew all the cowboys from the other saloons, including the Alamo which was owned by the mayor, Ab Webster. Mayor Webster had his council pass an ordinance prohibiting female piano players in Dodge saloons, and as soon as Luke Shore discharged the young lady, the mayor had the law repealed and gave her a job in the Alamo.

By the late Eighteen-seventies, Dodge's reputation was international, with half a million cattle moving through its shipping yards every year. And, as a veteran trail driver once declared: "Dodge was a town with the hair on!" One of the hotels, borrowing from Mark Twain, posted the following rules:

> This house will be considered strictly intemperate.
> None but the brave deserve the fare.
> Persons owing bills for board will be bored by bills.
> Sheets will be nightly changed once in six months—oftener if necessary.
> Boarders are expected to pull off their boots if they can conveniently do so.

During Dodge's first big season, twenty-four men were killed in gun battles. Its famed cemetery, Boot Hill, was founded in 1872 as a burial place for slow-triggered gentlemen and satin-slippered ladies. Among the interments recorded are such personages as Horse Thief Pete, Broad Mamie, Pecos Kid, and Toothless Nell.

Boot Hill was a rocky elevation northeast of Dodge. Other towns had their Boot Hills, but Dodge claims credit for first use of this term. According to Paul Wellman, the phrase "Red Light District" also originated in Dodge, red glass being used in the entrance of one of the favorite honkytonks, the old Red Light House south of the tracks. Other words still surviving in the American language which can be traced to Dodge are *stinker, stiff,* and *joint. Stinker* was first applied to buffalo hunters for their odor after handling partially rotted buffalo hides. *Stiff* was used to describe the frequently seen dead men lying on the streets. And the Dodge City *Times* originated the word *joint* in referring to the numerous saloons in the town.

To stop the practice of "killing a man for breakfast every morning," Dodge's solid citizens imported veteran peace officers from other trail towns. Wyatt Earp was town marshal for a time, and William Barclay (Bat) Masterson was sheriff of the county. The riding of animals into stores, saloons and dance halls was expressly forbidden.

But Dodge's reputation for wildness did not die easily. Newspapers in former trail towns fanned the legend with tall stories. In August, 1877, the Hays *Sentinel* reported that a dance hall girl tried to "horsewhip the editor of the Dodge City *Times* last week."

The Dodge City *Times* itself reported a similar incident during the same month: "Miss Frankie Bell who wears the belt for superiority in point of muscular ability, heaped epithets upon the unoffending head of Mr. Wyatt Earp to such an extent as to provoke a slap from the ex-officer, besides creating a disturbance of the quiet and dignity of the city, for which she received a night's lodging in the dog house and reception at the police court next morning, the expense of which was about $20. Wyatt Earp was assessed the lowest limit of the law, $1."

Floyd B. Streeter has told the story of the drunken cowboy who boarded the Santa Fe train at Newton. When the conductor asked for the fare, the cowboy handed him a fistful of money.

"Where do you want to go?" asked the conductor.

"To Hell," replied the cowboy.

"Well, give me $2.50 and get off at Dodge."

Some of the law dogs who finally tamed Dodge City were Mysterious Dave Mather, Bill Tilghman, Pat Sughrue, Frank McLean, Charlie Bassett, Bat Masterson, and his brother, Ed Masterson.

Bat Masterson was Dodge's favorite, a calm, well-dressed, blue-eyed man, an artist with a Colt forty-five and a veteran buffalo hunter. Before he came to Dodge, Bat was a civilian scout with the army. In a dance hall at Mobeetie, Texas, a jealous army sergeant shot and killed the girl with whom Bat was dancing, wounding Masterson in the leg. As he hit the floor, Bat pulled his gun and shot the sergeant through the heart. When the soldier's friends tried to mob Masterson, Ben Thompson came to his rescue. During his Dodge City days, Bat repaid Ben Thompson for the favor by rescuing his brother Bill Thompson from the wrathful citizens of Ogallala, Nebraska. Bill had been badly wounded, and the Ogallala citizens were waiting for him to recover so that they could hang him. Slipping into town secretly, Masterson engineered a sham battle in a dance hall just as a passenger train was pulling into Ogallala. During the commotion, Bat smuggled Bill out of his hotel bed and carried him to the train. Next morning they were in North Platte, where they stopped over at Buffalo Bill Cody's home until a team and stage could be commandeered into Dodge. It was a masterful escape.

On another occasion, Bat Masterson was called upon to protect a minor rascal, a certain Dr. Meredith who came to Dodge to lecture on phrenology and miscellaneous diseases. Having had rough experiences with cowboys in other trail towns, Dr. Meredith persuaded Bat to act as a sort of bodyguard during the lecture. The Lady Gay theater was rented for the evening, and Bat introduced the speaker to a large audience.

The good doctor began: "Ladies and gentlemen, I have been asked to—"

"You lie!" shouted a voice from the audience.

The doctor turned, glancing appealingly toward Sheriff Masterson. Bat stood up. "I'll shoot the first man that interrupts this gentleman again," he cried.

As soon as quiet was restored, the doctor began: "Several prominent citizens of Dodge—"

"You lie!" shouted the voice again.

Bat jumped up. "I meant what I said," he shouted. "The next time this gentleman is interrupted, I'll begin shooting."

99

Once again, Dr. Meredith started his speech. And a third time he was interrupted by the cry of the dubious listener.

Instantly Bat drew his revolver and shot out the lights. A crash sounded as a window was smashed. The Lady Gay was filled with yells, and other shots were fired. When the pandemonium ceased, Bat lighted a lamp. The Lady Gay was empty, except for Dr. Meredith, who was crouching under the speaker's stand. Some chroniclers of this event have implied that the entire affair was pre-arranged by Bat and the man in the audience. At any rate, Dr. Meredith's lecture was good for many a joke around the saloons of Dodge for the remainder of that shipping season.

Long after his tour of duty as sheriff, Bat Masterson became a friend of President Theodore Roosevelt, was appointed deputy United States Marshal in New York City, and ended his days as a sports writer on the *Morning Telegraph*.

Drawn to Dodge City by the romance of its living legend was Edward Fitzgerald, a New York stage comedian. Adopting the name of Eddie Foy, he first angered, then captivated the rugged but sentimental cowboys.

As Eddie Foy was arriving in Dodge City with his partner, Jim Thompson, he noted from the train window the enormous piles of buffalo bones. He thought the gunmen were killing people in Dodge faster than the bodies could be buried.

At first the cowboys resented Eddie's fancy clothing, his strut, and his jokes about them. In typical frontier fashion they roped and hauled him from the stage of the Comique (always pronounced Com-ee-cue in Dodge). Then they tied him to a horse and threatened to hang him from a tree. If he was frightened, Eddie Foy showed no evidence of it, continuing his jokes all the while. The cowboys liked his spirit, and for many months afterwards they packed the Comique Theater, begging for encores of Foy's specialty, *Kalamazoo in Michigan*.

Shows usually began at eight o'clock and lasted until after midnight. At one end of the hall, you could hear throughout the performances, the noise of the inveterate gamblers—the click and clatter of poker chips, balls, cards, dice, and wheels.

"All around the room," said Eddie Foy, describing the Comique, "up above, a sort of mezzanine, ran a row of private boxes—and they were boxes, indeed! As plain as a packing case!—where one might sit and drink and watch the show. When the various stage performances were over, there was dancing which might last until four A.M. or daybreak."

Another easterner also came to Dodge about this time, seeking fortune and fame of another kind. He was Elmo Z. C. Judson, who wrote blood-and-thunder fiction under the name of Ned Buntline. His dime novels about Buffalo Bill were winning a small fortune for both writer and subject.

Buntline sought out Wyatt Earp as a possible successor to the great Cody. Earp proved to be such a rich source of material that Buntline expressed his gratitude by presenting the marshal and his deputies with forty-five-caliber sixguns fitted with barrels twelve inches long. "Buntline Specials" they were called, with the word "Ned" carved in the handles.

100

Wyatt Earp once had to use his Buntline Special to tame Clay Allison of the Washita. Allison, credited with twenty-one killings, rode into Dodge purposely to smoke up the town, and to take Wyatt down a notch. Clay Allison had quite a reputation, too. In Canadian, Texas, he once stripped naked except for his holster and belt, then rode whooping through the main street. Allison was a Tennessean who never forgot that he fought on the Confederate side in the Civil War. He was six feet, six inches tall, quick as a cat, wore his wavy black hair long, had dark blue eyes, kept his short beard and mustache neatly trimmed. Fastidious in his dress, he affected contrasting blacks and whites, and usually rode either a white or a jet black horse.

When the dashing gunman rode into Dodge, he found Wyatt Earp standing in the entrance of the Long Branch Saloon. The two men exchanged less than a dozen words. Allison had his fingers around his revolver and had drawn it out of its holster, when he felt Earp's Buntline Special pressing into his ribs. It was just about a tie draw.

Earp backed slowly away.

"Reckon I'll be going," said Allison.

"Go ahead," replied Earp. "And don't come back."

But Clay Allison did come back a few days later, to prove he wasn't afraid of a Yankee peace officer. He transacted his cattle business in short order, and was not often a visitor to Dodge again.

Another Dodge City celebrity was John H. (Doc) Holliday. After he and Big Nose Kate Fisher had run afoul of the law and fled from Fort Griffin, Texas, they came to Dodge, which was just beginning its boom period as a trail town. Wyatt Earp took a liking to the gaunt, pale-faced Holliday, and in 1878 the gambler saved the marshal's life. When a band of cattle rustlers tried to gang Earp in the Long Branch Saloon, Holliday coolly stepped to the gun rack, removed his revolver, and broke up the party by shooting one of the rustlers in the shoulder. He then helped herd the outlaws across the street to the jail. Earp never forgot that incident. When he later went to Tombstone, Arizona, he took the sad-faced gambler with him, and there they fought together in one of the Southwest's bloodiest gun battles.

Dodge's mayor during its toughest years was a retired army sergeant, James H. Kelley, a former orderly of General George Custer, who for some reason became known as "Hound" Kelley in Hays City. When he moved to Dodge, he established with P. L. Beatty the Alhambra Saloon and Gambling House, and also operated the Dodge City Opera House and a dance hall. In Dodge, he was known as "Dog" Kelley.

Kelley loved animals and he kept for a pet a large black bear which one night broke its chain and crawled into bed with a drunken traveling man who was staying in the Dodge House. When the man awoke next morning, he took one look at the mayor's bear, then fled nightshirted into the dining room. After colliding with a waitress carrying a tray of dishes, the gentleman collapsed and thereafter swore off strong drink.

One of Mayor Kelley's good friends was Dora Hand, an actress whose real name was probably Fannie Keenan. Dora Hand sang with Eddie Foy on the stage of the Comique, and in several bars and honkytonks. More than one legend exists as to her

101

identity. Some said she was from an old Boston family. Others said she had sung in European opera. She was popular with both townsfolk and visiting cowmen, and frequently was invited to sing at weddings and funerals.

Dora Hand was living in a house owned by Dog Kelley when a feud between Kelley and Jim (Spike) Kennedy resulted in her tragic death in 1878. Believing Kelley to be asleep in the house, Kennedy fired into the actress' room, killing her instantly.

Dora's funeral was the most magnificent in Dodge's history. Instead of being buried on ignominious Boot Hill, her coffin was carried to Prairie Grove. Practically every dance hall girl, gambler, cowboy, gunman, business man and rancher in the vicinity followed the hearse to the cemetery.

Wyatt Earp and Bat Masterson chased Spike Kennedy for a hundred miles, captured him, and brought him back to Dodge for trial. Kennedy was freed, however, after he proved to the satisfaction of the judge that Dora Hand was not the person he had intended to kill.

BUFFALO HUNTERS' CAMP

> ". . . buffalo hump and iron wedge bread,
> All we had to sleep on was a buffalo robe for a bed."
> —The Buffalo Skinners.

Meanwhile an old trade of the western prairies was developing rapidly into a big business. On the western fringes of the shifting trail towns, the camps of the buffalo hunters were becoming more numerous. Small trading centers were established for the hunters, and these soon were mushrooming into towns.

BUFFALO CHASE

For centuries the buffalo had served as a source of food, clothing and shelter for the plains Indians. When the white men first pushed westward, and for many years afterwards, buffalo were considered unworthy of exploitation. Finally, when the fur trappers had practically exterminated the beaver and other animals, they turned to the buffalo for skins.

BUFFALO BILL CODY AND SITTING BULL (*on facing page*)

One of the greatest hunters was William F. Cody, who won his legendary name, Buffalo Bill, during this time. Many of the famed peace officers of the trail towns began their careers as buffalo hunters, including Wyatt Earp, Jack Bridges and William Barclay (Bat) Masterson.

MILLING A HERD

Experienced buffalo hunters knew how to fire so as to keep a herd milling, bringing a new target into place after each shot.

FIRST SOD HOUSE AT DODGE CITY (*on facing page, top*)

On the Sante Fe Trail five miles west of Fort Dodge, a sod house was erected in 1871 to serve the buffalo hunters. The place was known as Buffalo City. Standing in the doorway of the trading post above is Tom Nixon, who slew over two thousand buffalo in one month, probably an all-time record.

IRON HORSE COMES TO DODGE CITY (*on facing page*)

When the Sante Fe Railroad's construction gangs arrived in 1872, they found beside the old Sante Fe Trail a general store, three dance halls, and six saloons. The town now bore the name Dodge City, after Fort Dodge. Dodge, the old-timers called it, and they fondly hailed the place as "the cowboy capital." Dodge was also the last and longest-lived of all the Kansas trail towns.

BUFFALO HIDES AT DODGE CITY

This scene, probably sketched at Dodge City in 1874 by Paul Frenzeny and Jules Tavernier, shows an enormous business being done in buffalo hides. The huge pile in rear is a collection of buffalo bones, not considered to be of value until several years later.

BUFFALO HIDES AWAITING SHIPMENT (on facing page, top)

Wright & Rath were the largest shippers of buffalo hides in Dodge. This photograph shows forty thousand hides awaiting shipment to the eastern markets. Robert M. Wright is sitting on top of the pile.

IN THE BUFFALO COUNTRY (on facing page)

Other hide trading centers developed rapidly, such as the temporary dugout town shown above. In the heart of Texas' buffalo hunting grounds was Fort Griffin, a supply base for the hunters. Early cattle drivers on the Dodge City Trail usually funneled their cattle north through Fort Griffin, seeking protection from marauding Comanches.

109

TONKAWA INDIANS

Nearby were the Tonkawas, friendly Indians, who evidently believed the cattle herds were replacements for the buffalo killed by the white hunters. It was said that more beeves were lost to the friendly Tonkawas than to the unfriendly Comanches.

TRAIL DRIVERS "BUCKING THE TIGER"

Few cattle drivers passed Fort Griffin without a stopover. Gambling was the favorite relaxation, and faro was the popular game.

DOAN'S STORE ON RED RIVER

From Fort Griffin the drovers headed north, striking Red River at a place which came to be known as Doan's Crossing. Here, Judge C. F. Doan and his nephew, Corwin Doan, opened a large store, selling whiskey, guns, ammunition, saddles and blankets. It was a favorite stopping place for Texas cattlemen throughout the lifetime of the Western Trail.

JAMES H. COOK (*on facing page*)

One of the first cattlemen to make the long drive from Texas to the Dakotas was James H. Cook. In 1876, while still a young cow waddy, Cook helped drive a herd over the Western Trail from the Nueces River north to Dodge City, and then deep into the Sioux country.

113

NEW CATTLE ON A NEW TRAIL

Rumbling over this new trail to Dodge, and north into the Dakotas and Wyoming, was a new breed of cattle. The scrawny Longhorns were being replaced by Shorthorns and Herefords. "Whitefaces" instead of "Longhorns" were becoming the symbol of trail cattle.

DODGE CITY, FRONT STREET *(on facing page, top)*

This sprawling collection of false-front wooden buildings in Dodge City was a welcome sight to cowboys who had spent weeks driving cattle over miles of monotonous trails. The saloons and gambling dives seen here on Front Street between First and Second Avenues were settings for innumerable legends of Dodge's golden decade—including Beatty and Kelley's Alhambra Saloon, the Dodge Opera House, Delmonico's Restaurant, the Alamo and the Long Branch Saloon.

"BEAUTIFUL, BIBULOUS BABYLON OF THE PLAINS" *(on facing page)*

In the Long Branch Saloon, much of Dodge's violent history was acted out. Under its ornate chandeliers, Doc Holliday once saved Wyatt Earp's life. A celebrated faro dealer, Cockeyed Frank Loving, killed a gambler in a quick gunfight. And manager Luke Short employed here the first female pianist to perform in a Dodge saloon.

CATTLE AWAITING SHIPMENT
(on facing page, top)

Dodge was now the center of the cattle trade. Half a million cattle were moving through its shipping yards annually. When the season was at its height, the prairies south of town were covered with cattle as in this photograph taken in 1878.

DODGE'S PEACE COMMISSION
(on facing page)

"Dodge," said a veteran trail driver, "is a town with the hair on." During its first big season, twenty-four men were killed in gun battles. To stop the slaughter, Dodge's solid citizens imported veteran peace officers from other trail towns. Here are shown some of the law dogs of Dodge: *(top row, left to right)* Bill Harris, Luke Short, Bat Masterson. *(bottom row, left to right)* Charlie Bassett, Wyatt Earp, Frank McLean and Neal Brown.

EDDIE FOY *(on the right)*

Drawn to Dodge City by the romance of its living legend was Edward Fitzgerald, a New York stage comedian who called himself Eddie Foy. At first the cowboys resented Eddie's jokes about them, and one night they roped and hauled him from the stage of the theater. But Eddie knew how to win an audience, and he soon had his rugged listeners begging for encores every night.

TRAIL TOWN THEATER

The stage of a trail town theater was usually one end of a long hall filled with gambling tables. Shows began at eight o'clock, lasting until after midnight. Throughout the performances, one could hear the continual click and clatter of poker chips, roulette balls, cards, dice, and wheels.

NED BUNTLINE

Another easterner also came to Dodge about this time, seeking fame and fortune of another kind. He was Elmo Z. C. Judson, who wrote blood-and-thunder fiction under the name of Ned Buntline. The dime-novel author presented Wyatt Earp with a "Buntline Special," a six-gun fitted with a barrel twelve inches long.

CLAY ALLISON

Wyatt Earp once had to use his Buntline Special to tame Clay Allison of the Washita. Allison, credited with twenty-one killings, rode into Dodge purposely to smoke up the town and to take Wyatt down a notch. But Earp got the drop on him with his long-barreled six-gun, and Clay Allison went quietly on his way.

DOC HOLLIDAY

Another Dodge City celebrity was John H. (Doc) Holliday, a dentist turned gambler. Holliday once saved Wyatt Earp's life by shooting up a band of cattle rustlers who were trying to gang the marshal in the Long Branch Saloon. The two men became close friends, and later fought together in one of the southwest's bloodiest gun battles at Tombstone, Arizona.

MAYOR KELLEY (left) *AND CHARLIE HUNGERFORD*

Dodge's mayor during its toughest years was a retired army sergeant, James H. (Hound Dog) Kelley. Kelley had a pet bear which one night broke its chain and crawled into bed with a drunken traveling man who was staying in the Dodge House. When the man awoke next morning, he took one look at the mayor's bear, then fled nightshirted into the dining room where he collapsed. The gentleman thereafter swore off strong drink.

CHAPTER FIVE

The Beef Bonanza

One reason for the long reign of Dodge City as the cowboy capital was the development of a great new grazing area in the Texas Panhandle during the Eighteen-seventies.

Texas ranchers had known for a long time that this short grass country was ideal for cattle. With the passing of the great buffalo herds and the removal of the Comanches, a vast ocean of tufted velvet grass suddenly became open for ranching. In 1875, Fort Elliott was established on Sweetwater Creek as a deterrent to Indian raids from the north. That same year a rancher left Colorado and started driving remnants of his herd south to Texas. He was a victim of the Panic of 1873, and his name was Charles Goodnight.

Charles Goodnight's career as a cattleman had begun long before the Civil War. As a boy of eleven he rode a horse bareback from Illinois to Texas, and by 1857 was running a herd on the Palo Pinto range along the Brazos. When other Texans began driving their cattle north in 1866, Charles Goodnight decided to try the western market. He knew beef was scarce and brought high prices in New Mexico where there were many soldiers in army posts and many Indians on reservations.

Forming a partnership with Oliver Loving, he gathered a mixed herd of two thousand cows and steers. In June, 1866, the two partners and eighteen cow punchers started their historic drive over the abandoned route of Butterfield's Overland Mail.

For this hazardous journey, Charles Goodnight constructed what was probably the first chuckwagon. He bought the gear of a government wagon, and had it rebuilt with the toughest wood he knew, a wood used by the Indians for fashioning their bows—Osage Orange or *bois d'arc*. The wooden axles were replaced with iron, and for lubrication a can of tallow replaced the usual army tar bucket. Instead of horses he selected alternate teams of sturdy oxen to draw the wagon. At the rear of the bed he built a chuckbox with a hinged lid which dropped to form a cook's work table.

Driving south to avoid the Comanches, Goodnight and Loving forced their Longhorns for three days over eighty miles of the waterless Staked Plains to the Horsehead Crossing on the Pecos. When the thirsty herd smelled the river they became unmanageable. Several were drowned in the stampede, and so many dashed into the Pecos at once that the flow of the waters was blocked for a time.

After resting for three days, the herd swung north along the Pecos, fording the stream at Pope's Crossing, and then trailed on north to Fort Sumner. The gamble on the western drive paid off better than either Goodnight or Loving had expected. Although the government contractor at Fort Sumner would not take the eight hundred stocker cattle in the herd, he paid eight cents a pound on the hoof for the steers, a fabulous price in those days. The beef was needed to feed several thousand starving Navahos, recently placed in the government's keeping at Fort Sumner by the famous scout, Kit Carson.

While Goodnight hastily returned to Texas with twelve thousand dollars in gold to buy more cattle, Oliver Loving continued toward Denver, herding the unsold cows and calves. When Loving drove into the Raton Pass, he was stopped by a tollgate chain. The tollgate was guarded by a sly old scout named Richard Lacy Wootten, generally known as "Uncle Dick." Wootten had constructed a crude road through the pass and put up a tollgate and roadhouse. To Loving's chagrin, Uncle Dick demanded ten cents toll on each head of cattle. Loving probably got his money back, however, when he sold the herd for stocking to John W. Iliff of Colorado. The following year, while Charles Goodnight was driving another herd to Colorado, he had to pay the same toll. But in 1868 Goodnight outfoxed Uncle Dick by scouting a new route through Trincheras Pass.

The routes used by Goodnight and Loving soon became standard cattle trails to New Mexico and Colorado, and were known as the Horsehead Route and the Goodnight-Loving Trail.

The partnership of Oliver Loving and Charles Goodnight ended in 1867 after a tragic occurrence on the trail they had opened to New Mexico. Comanches attacked their herd near the Horsehead Crossing, stampeding most of the cattle. To further complicate matters, a thunderstorm broke suddenly. After a night of danger and confusion the trail drivers found the herd split into two sections, with Comanches on all sides.

Because of delays in rounding up the scattered Longhorns, Oliver Loving and "One-Armed Bill" Wilson rode toward Fort Sumner to notify the government contractor that the cattle would come through later than promised.

Riding only at night and hiding in the brush during the day, Loving and Wilson made fair progress for two days. At noon on the third day, Loving suggested that they continue without waiting for darkness. They had seen no Indians along the route, and no evidences of any recent raiding parties. But they had traveled only about ten miles when they saw a band of Comanches swarming down from the Guadalupe Mountains. Spurring their horses, the two men made a dash for the Pecos, and took cover in a brush-bordered ditch. They were armed with six-shooters and rifles, and carried considerable ammunition, but there were almost a hundred Indians in the party.

After surrounding Loving and Wilson, the Comanches began firing. Then as dark-

122

ness fell, one of the Indians called out in Spanish, proposing surrender terms. The trapped white men decided to talk. While Loving covered the rear, One-Armed Bill moved up into view of the enemy. Immediately a bullet crashed into Loving's hand and side. Wilson dropped back into the ditch cover, firing at the charging Indians until they retreated.

Loving took care of his wounds as best he could, but as night fell he grew too weak to help defend their position. Meanwhile the Comanches began dropping arrows perpendicularly into the ditch, at the same time showering the men with stones.

Believing that he was dying, Loving finally convinced Wilson that he should make an attempt to escape under cover of darkness. The escape of Wilson is one of the classics of western adventure. One-Armed Bill, carrying his long Henry rifle, crawled down the ditch to the river, where he saw mounted Comanches in the shallow stream waiting for him. Three times he attempted to pass them submerged; three times he withdrew, once because of the slight movement of a horse, twice because a cunning Comanche rider kept thrusting his foot down into the stream. Finally Wilson crawled under some overhanging brush along the bank and drifted in the mud until he was safe in the current beyond the watching Indians.

Through rocky, cactus-studded country, under a burning sun, he walked on foot for miles, always wary, until finally he met Charles Goodnight and the herd. Wilson's eyes were swollen, his feet cracked and bloody, and but for his one arm, Goodnight would not have recognized him.

A relief party was formed immediately, and with Goodnight leading rode hastily back to the scene of the fight on the Pecos. But when they reached the ditch where Wilson had left Loving, they found nothing but hundreds of arrow shafts and piles of stones hurled by the Comanches. Rainfall had obliterated all footprints. One-Armed Bill Wilson believed that Loving had shot himself and that his body had been thrown into the river by the Comanches. Everyone gave him up as dead.

But Oliver Loving was not dead. For two days he had held out against the Comanches, against the pain and fever of his wounds, against the gnawing pangs of hunger. The Indians showered him continually with stones and arrows, and even attempted to tunnel through the sand bank into his position. Finally on the third night of his stand, half-crazed with fever he crawled down to the river as Wilson had done, and miraculously escaped. For three more days he wandered. Once he stopped and tried to cook his buckskin gloves for food. He was in a stupor when a German immigrant boy and three Mexicans found him.

They took Loving to Fort Sumner, where several days later Charles Goodnight found him, standing inside the fort with one arm in a sling, watching the trail drivers come riding in. The pleasures of reunion, however, ended shortly afterwards. Gangrene affected Loving's arm, and the only doctor in Sumner was called upon to amputate it.

After the operation, Goodnight did not like the looks of the severed artery. He sent a man on relays of horses all the way to Las Vegas for a trained surgeon. But nothing could save Oliver Loving. He died after securing a promise from his partner to have his body removed to Texas.

Goodnight kept his word. He ordered the cowboys to gather empty oil cans from the fort's dumping ground, and had them flattened and soldered together to form a tin coffin. In this crude casket, Oliver Loving went home to Texas over the trail he had helped to blaze.

With Oliver Loving gone, Charles Goodnight continued his cattle drives to Colorado. In 1868 he made a drive to Cheyenne, selling his herd to John W. Iliff. He ranged cattle in New Mexico on the Bosque Grande, an area later taken over by John Chisum, a man to be linked later with the name of Billy the Kid. The two men were friends, and Goodnight trailed thousands of Chisum's cattle northward.

During the winter of 1869, Goodnight selected a sheltered valley on the Arkansas River above Pueblo, and decided to locate his home ranch there. The next year he married Mary Ann Dyer, and for three years prospered as a Colorado rancher, irrigation promoter, and banker. But the Panic of 1873, in Goodnight's words, "wiped me off the face of the earth." He spent two years trying to recover, then turned back to Texas for the greatest venture of his life.

He remembered the unbroken miles of grass on the Staked Plains, recalled canyons, springs, small streams he had seen at scattered intervals. He knew that most of the buffalo were gone, and that the danger of the Comanches was now practically ended.

After assembling a herd of about two thousand cattle in the autumn of 1875, he accepted as volunteer assistant on the drive, James T. Hughes, an Englishman who had come to the United States to learn the business of ranching. He was the son of Thomas Hughes, author of *Tom Brown's Schooldays*. Another partner was J. C. Johnston, a Scotchman, later director of the Matador Land and Cattle Company. Hughes and Johnston were the pioneers of a small army of British adventurers who would in the next few years assume dominant roles in the development of the cattle trade.

During Goodnight's drive south toward the Texas Panhandle, James Hughes proved to be an excellent cowpuncher, and he found time to keep a diary of the journey.

The army was operating extensively across their path, and loose bands of Indians were everywhere. Goodnight decided to make winter camp near Fort Bascom in New Mexico. He was not certain of his exact destination, and needed plenty of time. He knew he wanted to locate his new ranch somewhere on the Staked Plains south of the Canadian, but was not sure of the best place.

In the spring of 1876, he started the herd drifting slowly down the Canadian. They moved into the Panhandle, and near Tascosa crossed the river. Here a Mexican trader, Nicolas Martinez, helped Goodnight decide on his ranch site. Martinez had wandered into the cow camp, and during a conversation with Goodnight chanced to speak of the Palo Duro Canyon, an enormous grassy valley where Chief Lone Wolf had once made a stand against the cavalry. Goodnight employed the Mexican as a guide, and they went ahead to see the Palo Duro. As soon as the two men rode up to the edge of the canyon, Goodnight knew it was the place he had been seeking.

Buffalo grass carpeted the valley of the canyon, but to reach the grazing area from the plain the cattle had to be driven single file down an old Indian trail. Goodnight's cherished chuckwagon was taken apart and lowered by lariats.

In the canyon, they found ten thousand buffalo feeding upon the luxuriant grass. Goodnight and his men chased them out, but a guard had to be maintained at the entrance of the canyon to keep the buffalo from returning to this choice feeding ground.

Probably nowhere else could have been found such a natural location for a ranch. No fencing was needed, water was plentiful, the grass was like a velvety green sea. Goodnight named it the Old Home Ranch. It was the first in the Panhandle.

When Goodnight returned to Colorado for his wife, he met John G. Adair, a wealthy Irishman. Adair offered to finance the cattleman in a mammoth venture, and the million-acre ranch which resulted became the famed JA, after Adair's initials.

After the splendid ranch buildings were completed in the Palo Duro Canyon, the Adairs occasionally came to Texas for inspections. Cornelia Wadsworth Adair usually brought a trainload of personal baggage, dozens of maids and butlers, and all the luxuries of the East. What Charles Goodnight thought of these early attempts at dude ranching is not recorded. Perhaps he was not surprised when Mrs. Adair, after her husband's death, became one of the best ranch managers in Texas.

The JA flourished from its beginnings. Goodnight introduced Durhams, the early Shorthorns, but they were unsuited to that country. Herefords proved to be so successful, however, they were given a special brand, the JJ. In five years, the Goodnight-Adair partnership realized a profit of over half a million dollars.

But after eleven years, Charles Goodnight withdrew from the JA. He was ready to finance his own ranch now. Sixty miles from the Old Home Ranch, he selected a ranging area along the Fort Worth & Denver City Railroad. The town which developed near his headquarters was named Goodnight.

One of the experiments he conducted on this ranch was the cross-breeding of buffaloes and cattle. The calves were named cattaloes, but they were unsuccessful as meat producers. He also found time to design a saddle for western women. In those days no lady straddled a horse; she rode sidesaddle on a piece of eastern gear strictly unsuited for lively range ponies. After witnessing an accident, Goodnight decided to design a safe sidesaddle, and he persuaded his favorite saddle-maker, S. C. Gallup of Pueblo, Colorado, to manufacture a few for sale. The Goodnight sidesaddle was popular immediately, and came into general use in the West.

As he grew older, Charles Goodnight insisted on strict rules for his men. Card playing and liquor drinking were taboo. He particularly disliked mumblepeg, a harmless but time-consuming game popular with the cowboys. Determined to break up mumblepeg, Goodnight asked the Panhandle Cattlemen's Association to forbid the game on all ranches.

Goodnight's punchers either loved him or hated him; they all worked hard to please him. His drives to Dodge City were leisurely marches, so well organized that his steers gained weight on the trail. When range fencing began in the Eighteen-eighties, he purchased the best equipment on the market, insisted that each post be set like a rock.

On a diet consisting chiefly of meat and black coffee, and sometimes a box of cigars per day, Charles Goodnight lived to be ninety-three, one of the last of the giants of the old cattle trails. He died in 1929.

Charles Goodnight had pioneered the development of the Panhandle, but a cavalry soldier named James S. Brisbin probably had more influence in generating the beef bonanza of the Eighteen-eighties than any other single human being.

Before the Civil War, James Brisbin was a Pennsylvania schoolmaster and country newspaper editor. He joined up with the Union Army in 1861 at the age of twenty-four, and four years later he was a brevet-general. Brisbin liked army life, and after the war he went West with the Indian-fighting cavalry. During his movements from post to post on the plains, he got a first-hand view of the rapidly expanding cattle trade. He saw fortunes made in a single season, and after years of army service for scanty pay, he was tremendously impressed by the cattlemen who could drive a herd into a reservation and depart the next day with a bag full of money.

General Brisbin figured all the angles, on paper. He sent enthusiastic reports to *Wilkes's Spirit of the Times,* a widely circulated sporting journal. Finally he wrote a book, *The Beef Bonanza, or How to Get Rich on the Plains,* published in 1881. The book had a good sale in this country, and a phenomenal sale in Britain.

To say that Brisbin's prose fascinated his British readers would be an understatement. They were hypnotized by such passages as the following:

"The West! The mighty West! That land where the buffalo still roams and the wild savage dwells: where the broad rivers flow and the boundless prairie stretches away for thousands of miles; where new States are every year carved out and myriads of people find homes and wealth . . . where there are lands for the landless, money for the moneyless. . . .

"If $250,000 were invested in ten ranches and ranges, placing 2,000 head on each range, by selling the beeves as fast as they mature, and all the cows as soon as they were too old to breed well, and investing the receipts in young cattle, at the end of five years there would be at least 45,000 head on the ten ranges, worth at least $18 per head, or $810,000. . . . I have no doubt but a company properly managed would declare an annual dividend of at least 25 per cent. . . ."

It seemed that every Briton with money to invest was reading Brisbin's book. Several of them had already visited the American West to shoot buffalo, and had seen the possibilities of ranching. Brisbin's *Beef Bonanza* met an unusually receptive public.

One of the first British companies to be formed was the Prairie Cattle Company, Ltd., and it opened the era of big-money ranching in the Panhandle in 1882 with the purchase of Thomas Bugbee's Quarter Circle T for the startling price of $350,000.

Shortly after the establishment of the JA in Palo Duro Canyon, Thomas Bugbee and his wife Molly had driven a small herd down from Kansas, moving into a dugout near Adobe Walls on the Canadian. It was the first headquarters of the Quarter Circle T. Molly Bugbee had insisted on bringing along a wooden door, and they used buffalo robes for carpeting the earthen floor. Six years later, the Bugbees sold out to the Prairie Cattle Company for that unbelievable sum of $350,000.

In 1877, a year after the Bugbees settled on the Canadian, Major George W. Littlefield sent a large herd up the trail from central Texas to Dodge City, but the market was

126

glutted that season. Littlefield's trail boss drifted the unsold herd back into the open range of the Panhandle, setting up winter headquarters near Tascosa.

Here was established the LIT, one of the largest "squatter" ranches in Texas. Littlefield never claimed any land rights, but four years later he sold his equipment and stock to the British-financed Prairie Cattle Company for more than $125,000.

"That outfit owns all outdoors," Texas cattlemen were now saying of the Prairie Cattle Company. It seemed the British had no end of money. In 1885 they offered Henry W. Creswell one and a half million dollars for his Bar CC, north of the Canadian. They bought up the Cross L's and the JJ Ranch in New Mexico. Within three years, the Prairie Cattle Company had acquired an unbroken range from the Canadian River in Texas to the Arkansas River in Colorado.

Other British investors were also coming into the Panhandle. On 500,000 acres in Dickens, Kent, Crosby and Garza counties, the Spur Ranch was founded for the express purpose of resale to British capitalists, who were so eager to invest in the Beef Bonanza. As grazing areas became scarce, the Scotch and English promoters seemed to become more avid than ever. The fad was "to buy at once and repent at leisure." So, in 1882, a group of smart stockmen headed by Colonel A. M. Britton of Colorado organized the Spur, and sold it two years later to a London syndicate at more profit than the absentee owners earned over the next two decades.

And in 1883 the Rocking Chair Ranche Company was formed, a remarkable organization. Principal shareholders were James Gordon, the Earl of Aberdeen, and Edward Marjoribanks, Baron Tweedmouth. "Little England" was soon established in the Panhandle, between the North and Salt Forks of Red River. Headquarters was known as Aberdeen. The Britishers called their punchers "cow servants." The cowboys dubbed the place "Nobility Ranch," and in a few months every outfit in the neighborhood was mavericking cattle from the inefficient Rocking Chair.

Archibald John Marjoribanks, a young relative of Baron Tweedmouth, arrived from London to set things in order. He brought over some English horses, and the cowboys immediately dubbed them "peckernecks." When young Marjoribanks ordered the punchers to address him as Sir Archibald, they rebelled. They took to hiding out on the range where they would wait for Marjoribanks to come galloping by on his English saddle with his scissors-tail coat flying; then the cowboys would charge him, firing off their pistols and whooping like Indians.

One day, according to Panhandle legend, Aberdeen and Tweedmouth arrived incognito to find out why the ranch was earning no profits. Although Tweedmouth personally supervised the cattle count, his manager tricked the nobleman by driving the same herd past him several times.

Rustling from the Rocking Chair grew so common that the Englishmen's bloodhounds had to be pressed into service to round up the few cattle left on the sprawling range. When the owners finally sold out, their books showed fourteen thousand head belonging to the ranch. But the final roundup produced only three hundred.

Another ranch that was big and rich from its beginnings was the LX. D. T. Beals and W. H. Bates of Boston pooled their resources and soon had the added backing of a wealthy Scotch-English company for a 200,000-acre range near Tascosa. Charlie Siringo was a cowhand on the LX, and helped drive thousands of fat cattle up the trail to Dodge every season. Siringo later became a range detective, and after his retirement he wrote several books about his adventures.

When Billy the Kid rustled some steers off the LX, Charlie Siringo and a group of punchers from neighboring ranches went into New Mexico in hot pursuit. They recovered some of the cattle, but the elusive Kid got away as usual. William C. (Bill) Moore was the first LX foreman, and he also helped chase Billy the Kid away from the ranch. But later, Moore was suspected of mavericking from the LX himself. In three years he built up a herd which he sold for $70,000, a large sum for a man on top hand's wages. Moore left the LX hastily and disappeared. Many years afterwards Charlie Siringo saw him in Juneau, Alaska, but Bill Moore refused to admit his identity.

One of the mail drivers on the stage route from Tascosa to Dodge City was a young man named Cape Willingham. He had learned to punch cattle under Charles Goodnight, and had served for a while as a cowboy detective on the LX when Bill Moore was under suspicion for rustling. Later he became sheriff of the county dominated by Tascosa.

When the Hansford Land and Cattle Company established the huge Turkey Track Ranch near historic Adobe Walls in 1883, Cape Willingham was chosen to boss the outfit. For twenty years he was also the "boss" of that section of the Panhandle, carrying a sawed-off shotgun that stood for law and order. He built for his wife the first frame house in Hutchinson County from lumber hauled all the way from Dodge City. He liked to play poker with his cowboys, and was fond of horse racing. Willingham was once tried for murder as the result of the shooting of a "nester" believed to be a cattle thief, but he received a quick and complete acquittal.

One night in 1878, Henry H. Campbell was attending a banquet in Chicago. He had just sold a herd of cattle at twenty-three dollars a head, cattle that had cost him nine dollars in Texas. By the time his story got around the banquet table, a new cattle company was being formed. H. H. Campbell went back to Texas with $50,000 to found the Matador Ranch in the southern Panhandle.

Campbell bought up a ranging area southeast of the JA headquarters below the Prairie Dog Fork of Red River. His first ranch house was a dugout; his first cattle came from John Chisum's New Mexico range. As soon as the Matador was well organized, Campbell and his wife gave a Christmas ball, inviting all the ranchers and cowboys within a hundred miles. For years, the Matador's Christmas ball was an annual event in the lower Panhandle.

Not long after the ranch was established, Scotch financiers backed an expansion program, and soon the Matador was spreading over the entire Panhandle, even into Montana. Thanks to the efficient management of Henry H. Campbell and his successors, Murdo Mackenzie, Frank Mitchell, and other great cattlemen, the Matador survived droughts, blizzards, and depressions. It was operated by its original owners longer than any other ranch in the Panhandle.

Long before the Panhandle was opened for ranching, a farmer in De Kalb, Illinois, was trying to invent a method for manufacturing barbed wire. The farmer's name was Joseph F. Glidden, and finally in 1874, using an old coffee grinder, Glidden manufactured the first coil barb. The effect of this invention on the Panhandle and all open ranges was such that in a very few years the entire cattle trade was transformed. Barbed wire meant the end of free grass forever.

At first Glidden could not sell his barbed wire to cattlemen, who feared that it would harm their stock. Such influential ranchers as Shanghai Pierce were determined to have nothing to do with it; they said the barbed wire would cut up their cattle and the injured animals would all die of screw worms. When the Texas legislature threatened to make the wire illegal, two extraordinary salesmen, Henry B. Sanborn and John (Bet-a-Million) Gates, were sent as missionaries into the ranching country.

A barbed wire corral was built in the main plaza of San Antonio, and a bunch of Longhorns were placed inside it. The Texas cowmen were soon convinced the wire would hold cattle satisfactorily and without injury. To prove further the advantages of barbed wire, Glidden and Sanborn established the first barbed-wire enclosed ranch in the Panhandle, on Tecoras Creek in Potter County. Their brand was designed as a Panhandle, but to cowboys the design looked more like a Frying Pan. From the Frying Pan's activities developed the town of Amarillo, now the largest city in the Panhandle.

On Glidden's first visit to the ranch, he was asked: "What do you think of our country, Mr. Glidden?"

"Country's all right," said he, "but there's not enough grass to feed a goose." He did not know that the short yellow-gray, sun-cured grass of the Panhandle was as good forage for beef cattle as the green grass of his Illinois farmland.

When a brisk Texas wind swept off Glidden's high-topped silk hat, a cowboy had to retrieve it with a lariat. Glidden soon returned to De Kalb where his partner, Isaac Elwood, was having troubles with their barbed wire patents.

Strangely enough, the burning of the Texas state capitol in 1881 started a chain of events which led to the greatest barbed wire fencing project in history. Texans demanded that their new capitol be the biggest in the United States, with a dome at least one foot higher than that of the national capitol in Washington. To get it they traded 3,000,000 acres of Panhandle land to a Chicago group of contractors and financiers.

The Texas legislators who made the swap thought they had the better of the bargain until John and Charles Farwell of a Chicago syndicate formed the Capitol Freehold Land and Investment Company. The Farwells proceeded to wind eight hundred miles of barbed wire around their holdings and soon had the biggest ranch going in the Panhandle.

The ranch was called the XIT, supposedly meaning "ten in Texas" for the ten counties from which the land had been surveyed. Actually there were only nine counties, and Ab Blocker who designed the brand said he picked XIT because "it looked good, sounded good, and was easy to put on." Blocker, a veteran trail driver, never worked for the XIT, but when he brought in the first cattle to the ranch on July 1, 1885, the resident manager, B. H. (Barbecue) Campbell asked him to help design a suitable brand. With his boot heel, Blocker slowly marked off the letters XIT on the ground. While trying out the design on a couple of steers, Blocker was informed that the old method of throwing cattle before branding was frowned on by the ranch owners. They wanted all their stock chute-branded.

Next day, Barbecue Campbell offered Blocker a job on the XIT, but the trail driver declined immediately. "I don't want to work for a ranch that don't know how to brand cattle," said Blocker.

When Barbecue Campbell resigned, following a dispute over policies with the XIT owners, A. G. Boyce became general manager. The XIT ranch soon became so large it was cut into eight divisions, each with a foreman and each designed for a specific function; some for breeding, some for young stock, some for top grade cattle, and so forth.

Boyce ruled the enormous area for eighteen years, controlling politics in several counties, enforcing the company's unpopular rules against drinking, gambling, and the carrying of firearms. Even the traditional hospitality of the range was forbidden. Travelers crossing the XIT holdings, or riders from other outfits visiting an XIT chuckwagon, were charged for their meals. A. G. Boyce knew that the Panhandle disapproved of XIT policies, but he had his orders and he carried them out to the letter. He was happiest organizing long drives to the XIT pastures in Montana, each year sending about twelve thousand cattle up the Montana Trail through eastern Colorado and Wyoming to Miles City. These were the last great cattle drives from Texas.

XIT cowboys fared better than the average. One division foreman always supplied his men on range and trail duty with ham, eggs, and even butter, a chuckwagon diet undreamed of before the coming of the XIT.

At the peak of its operations, the great ranch was running cattle on a two-hundred-mile range in Texas, on a two-hundred-mile range in Montana, and was trailing them over the twelve hundred miles of the Montana Trail. No other ranch ever equaled this geographic record. Its stockholders, however, never received a penny in dividends from ranching operations. At the turn of the century, the company began selling its acreage to small ranchers and to farmers, and the XIT was no more.

Favorite haunt for off-duty cowboys in the Panhandle was old Tascosa, where Charles Goodnight had crossed the Canadian on his pioneering venture in 1876. Tascosa developed rapidly after the coming of the ranches. The town lay in a shady cottonwood grove above the river, and during roundup seasons it became a little "Dodge City," with its Frog Lip Sadies, Rowdy Kates, Panhandle Nans, Midnight Roses, and Box Car Janes.

Billy the Kid made Tascosa his temporary headquarters on several occasions. During one visit, the Kid, Bat Masterson, and Temple Houston, son of the great Sam Houston, engaged in a polite target-shooting match before a large crowd of spectators. For the glory of Texas, Temple Houston won the match and the Kid's congratulations. The Kid was usually on his best behavior while in Tascosa. He used the town as a sort of hideout after stirring up hornet's nests in New Mexico.

But other outlaws were not so well behaved. Tascosa's Boot Hill filled up rapidly in the early Eighteen-eighties. The town's bloodiest gun battle occurred one night in March, 1886, when four LS cowboys rode into Tascosa looking for fun and pleasure. One of them became involved in a quarrel over a dance hall girl and was killed on the street. His three companions pulled their guns, and in a few seconds two of them and one Tascosa resident were dead. Tascosans had a big burying in Boot Hill next day.

The XIT, which had begun to dominate Tascosa, disapproved of such violent practices, and the growth of that businesslike ranch had also doomed the colorful trading town. The XIT fence across 260 miles of land to the north and west of Tascosa soon cut off free access from New Mexico, and the rough-riding punchers from those parts would come no more to h'ist the tarantula juice and lay the dust in their throats.

Tascosa's principal rival in the Panhandle was Mobeetie, a hundred miles to the east on Sweetwater Creek. Mobeetie grew up beside Fort Elliott in the early days of the cattle trade, and its citizens claimed they could raise more hell any day of the week than the inhabitants of Tascosa.

Clarendon, on the other hand, was a highly moral town. No saloons were permitted, but thanks to the paternal protection of Charles Goodnight and other ranchers who liked to keep their cowboys sober, Clarendon prospered. The punchers called it "Saint's Roost." Extreme penalty of the Tascosa court was the sentence ordering offenders "to spend a week in Clarendon."

For a short time after the closing of the range in the Panhandle, Clayton, New Mexico, just west of the Texas line, served as a trail driving point on the new Denver & Fort Worth Railroad. But Clayton's career as a trail town was short-lived. Range fencing recognized no state lines.

Meanwhile Dodge City had grown prosperous catering to the Texans, prosperous and perhaps "dandified" as some of the old-timers charged. There was less violence; more concern with cattle prices. In July 1884, some of the early settlers tried to revive the old spirit by staging the first bullfight in the United States.

But Dodge was sophisticated now. A fancy cowboy band was organized to play for the cattlemen's conventions. The band toured in the East, marching in President Benjamin Harrison's inaugural parade. When a newspaper reporter asked J. W. Eastman, the director, why he carried a six-shooter, Eastman replied: "It's my baton."

"Is it loaded?" asked the reporter. "Yes," said Eastman. "What for?" continued the reporter. "To kill the first man who strikes a false note," replied Eastman.

Symptoms of the great cowtown's waning glory were already apparent. Land office business was booming. The "fool hoe men" were on every side. And instead of herding cattle, these new settlers were rounding up jack rabbits.

As early as 1879, Wyatt Earp decided that Dodge was too tame for him. At the end of the season that year, he and Doc Holliday and Big Nose Kate Fisher left for Tombstone, Arizona.

In 1884, cattlemen from the range country suddenly became so concerned over the rapid extension of fences and the growing power of the grangers, that they gathered for a convention in St. Louis. Trail drivers everywhere had discovered there were no more open trails to market. They called their meeting the First National Cattle Growers Con-

131

vention. Ranchers from Texas and the Southwest demanded a National Livestock Trail, to be established by law, extending from Red River to the Canadian border. It was to be three miles wide, with grazing areas at intervals, and was to be fenced all the way.

The National Livestock Trail died in St. Louis. A Texas Congressman introduced a bill in the House of Representatives, but the grangers and the railroads opposed it firmly, and the northwestern cattlemen gave it no support.

The day of the Texas trail driver was coming to an end.

With the closing of the trails, Dodge City's golden splendor declined rapidly. Even during its best years, cattlemen had occasionally driven herds past Dodge's shipping yards to Ogallala, Nebraska, on the Union Pacific Railroad; and now as Dodge declined, Ogallala boomed. The trainloads of beef from this little town on the Platte were soon creating a new packing center in Omaha.

But Ogallala was only a transition point, a brief moment in the great swing of open range cattle ranching from southwest to northwest. The Beef Bonanza which had transformed the Panhandle had also been developing the great plains of Wyoming and Montana.

The last great trail drives from the Southwest were not drives to markets, but were emigrations from a closed range to the last great open range in the United States. Thousands of picked young cattle had been going north to flood the grasslands of Wyoming and Montana, the sacred hunting grounds lost by the fighting Sioux and Cheyennes in the late Eighteen-seventies. Here, like the Indians, the free range cattlemen would make their last stand.

CHARLES GOODNIGHT

When other Texas cattlemen began driving their herds north in 1866, Charles Goodnight decided to try the western market. He had heard that beef was scarce and brought high prices in New Mexico. Forming a partnership with Oliver Loving, he gathered a herd of two thousand cattle, and in June, 1866, the two partners started their historic drive over the abandoned route of Butterfield's Overland Mail. The route would soon be known as the Goodnight-Loving Trail.

CHUCKWAGON ON THE MOVE
For this historic journey, Charles Goodnight constructed what was probably the first chuckwagon. Using tough Osage Orange wood, he rebuilt an old army wagon. A chuckbox with a hinged lid was fastened to the rear of the bed.

CHUCKBOX

Duplicates of Goodnight's chuckwagon were soon seen on all the ranges and along the cattle trails. And to this day, the wagon has changed very little, still carrying the chuckbox with its hinged lid and compartments, and up front the cowboy's bedrolls, and the simple tools needed on the range.

FORT SUMNER, NEW MEXICO

Driving south to avoid the Comanches, Goodnight and Loving forced their Longhorns over the waterless Staked Plains to the Horsehead Crossing on the Pecos, and swung north to Fort Sumner. The gamble paid off. At Fort Sumner, they sold twelve hundred cattle to a government contractor for premium prices.

UNCLE DICK WOOTTEN

While Goodnight returned to Texas to buy more cattle, Oliver Loving continued towards Denver with the eight hundred unsold animals. In the Raton Pass, Loving was stopped by a tollgate. The chain was guarded by a sly old scout, Uncle Dick Wootten, who demanded ten cents toll on each head of cattle. Loving paid the fee, but two years later Charles Goodnight outfoxed Uncle Dick by scouting a new route through Trincheras Pass.

WILLIS HOLLOWAY

Willis Holloway was one of the drivers for Goodnight and Loving. A seasoned trail man, Holloway had driven cattle from Texas to California before the Civil War.

On one drive over the Horsehead Route, when a bandit party from Mexico attempted to steal some of the cattle, Goodnight was attacked with knives. Holloway came to his rescue and stood the bandits off with a pistol.

OLIVER LOVING

The partnership of Oliver Loving and Charles Goodnight ended in 1867, when Loving was wounded and trapped by Comanches. Loving miraculously escaped from the Indians, but he died soon after reaching Fort Sumner. For more than sixty years, Charles Goodnight kept Loving's photograph (*above*) on his ranch house wall.

COLORADO RANCH

In 1870, Goodnight established a ranch in Colorado, near Pueblo. He prospered for three years; then the Panic of 1873, in his own words "wiped me off the face of the earth." To obtain a new start, he decided to return to Texas.

IN PALO DURO CANYON

For his Texas ranch site, Goodnight selected the Palo Duro Canyon in the heart of the Staked Plains. Probably nowhere else could he have found such a natural location for a ranch. The canyon walls served as fencing, water was plentiful, the grass was like a rippling sea of velvet. Goodnight named it the Old Home Ranch. It was the first in the Panhandle.

CORNELIA WADSWORTH ADAIR

John G. Adair, wealthy Irishman, financed the development of Goodnight's ranch, and the million-acre venture which followed was named the J A, for Adair's initials. Cornelia Wadsworth Adair was a frequent visitor, usually bringing a trainload of baggage and servants. After her husband's death, Mrs. Adair surprised some of her critics by becoming one of the best ranch managers in Texas.

J A RANCH SCENE

The J A flourished from its beginnings. Charles Goodnight introduced Durhams, the early Shorthorns, but they were unsuited to that country. Herefords proved to be so successful, however, they were given a special brand, the J J. In five years the Goodnight-Adair partnership realized a profit of over half a million dollars.

COWBOYS AT PLAY

As he grew older, Goodnight insisted on strict rules for his men. Card playing and liquor drinking were taboo. He particularly disliked mumblepeg, a time-consuming game popular with the cowboys.

CATTALO AND SIDE SADDLE (*on facing page*)

After eleven years, Charles Goodnight withdrew from the J A, establishing a ranch along the new Fort Worth & Denver City Railroad. For a time he experimented with the cross-breeding of buffaloes and cattle. The calves were called "cattaloes," but they were unsuccessful as meat producers. He also found time to develop a safe side-saddle for western women, who in those days did not ride astride their mounts.

143

CHARLES GOODNIGHT IN LATER YEARS

On a diet consisting chiefly of meat and black coffee, and sometimes a box of cigars per day, Charles Goodnight lived to be ninety-three, one of the last of the giants of the old cattle trails. He died in 1929.

THE BEEF BONANZA

Brisbin's book, published in 1881, had a powerful influence on the development of the western cattle trade, and heralded the era of big money ranching in the Panhandle.

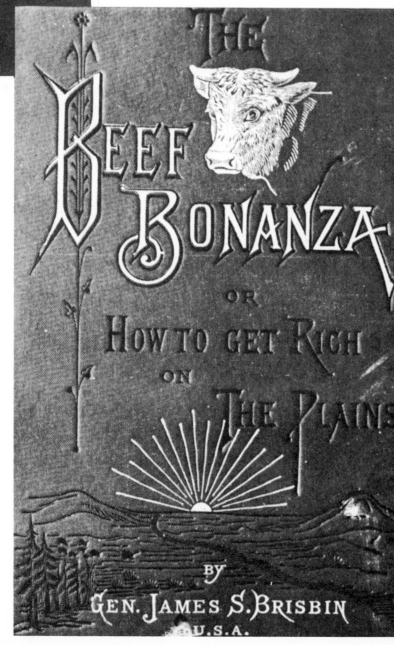

GEORGE W. LITTLEFIELD
AND L I T COWBOYS

In 1877, Major George W. Littlefield sent up a large herd from central Texas to Dodge City, but the market was glutted that season. Littlefield's trail boss drifted the unsold herd back into the open range of the Panhandle, setting up winter headquarters near Tascosa. Here was established the L I T, one of the largest "squatter" ranches in Texas.

H. H. CAMPBELL

One night in 1878, H. H. Campbell was attending a banquet in Chicago. He had just sold a herd of cattle at twenty-three dollars a head, cattle that had cost him nine dollars in Texas. By the time his story got around the banquet table, a new cattle company was being formed. H. H. Campbell went back to Texas with fifty-thousand dollars to found the Matador Ranch in the southern Panhandle.

MATADOR COWBOYS

A short time later, Scotch financiers backed an expansion program for the Matador, and soon the ranch was spreading over the Panhandle. (This photo was made by Erwin E. Smith on the Matador range. Smith secretly set his camera and then threw a handful of flash powder on the campfire just as Billy Partlow, the Pitchfork Kid, was telling a good one.)

SPUR RANCH

On five hundred thousand acres in four Panhandle counties, the Spur Ranch was organized in 1882. Two years later it was sold to a London syndicate at more profit than the absentee owners earned over the next two decades. (Above photograph is of Dave Carter on his horse Butterbean during the last roundup of Spur cattle, after the ranch was sold to Swenson Brothers' SMS in 1907.)

CHARLIE SIRINGO (*on facing page*)

Charlie Siringo was a cowhand on the LX, a two hundred thousand acre ranch near Tascosa, backed by a Boston-London-Edinburgh combine. From his experiences, Siringo wrote *A Texas Cowboy,* one of the great classics of the American West.

149

WILLIAM C. (BILL) MOORE

Bill Moore, the first LX foreman, was suspected of mavericking steers from his own ranch. Moore left the LX hastily and disappeared. Many years later, Charlie Siringo saw him in Alaska, but Bill Moore refused to admit his identity.

DODGE-TASCOSA LINE
AND
CAPE WILLINGHAM

One of the mail drivers on the stage route from Tascosa to Dodge City was Cape Willingham. When the Hansford Land and Cattle Company established the huge Turkey Track Ranch near Adobe Walls in 1883, Cape Willingham was chosen to boss the outfit.

PRAIRIE CATTLE COMPANY, LTD.

"That outfit owns all outdoors," Texas cattlemen were soon saying of the Prairie Cattle Company, Ltd. By 1885, this British combine acquired an unbroken range from the Canadian River in Texas to the Arkansas River in Colorado. Above are two of the managers of the company: Murdo Mackenzie, seated *center;* and W. J. Tod, *right.* Henry Johnston is standing, and a Mr. Hopkins is on the *left.*

JOSEPH F. GLIDDEN

As the Panhandle was being opened to ranching, Joseph F. Glidden in DeKalb, Illinois, was perfecting his invention for manufacturing barbed wire. The effect of barbed wire on the open range would be tremendous —it would mean the end of free grass forever.

JOHN AND CHARLES FARWELL

The burning of the Texas state capitol in 1881 started a chain of events which led to the greatest barbed wire fencing project in history. In exchange for building a new capitol, John and Charles Farwell received three million acres of Panhandle land. The Farwells wound eight hundred miles of barbed wire around their holdings and soon had the biggest ranch going in the Panhandle.

AB BLOCKER AND FRIENDS

The ranch was called the XIT. Ab Blocker, veteran trail driver, designed the brand. He said he picked XIT because it "looked good, sounded good, and was easy to put on." (In photo above, *left to right:* Captain John R. Hughes, famous Texas Ranger, Ellison Carroll, Ab Blocker, and Bob Beverly.)

CHUTE BRANDING

While trying out the new XIT brand on a couple of rambunctious steers, Ab Blocker was informed that the old method of throwing cattle to the ground before branding was against the rules of the ranch owners. They wanted all their stock chute-branded.

Next morning when Barbecue Campbell offered Blocker a job on the XIT, the trail driver declined immediately. "I don't want to work for a ranch that don't know how to brand cattle," said Blocker.

A. G. BOYCE

A. G. Boyce ruled the enormous area for eighteen years as general ranch manager. He controlled politics in several counties, organized long drives to the XIT pastures in Montana, and enforced the company's unpopular rules against drinking, gambling, and the carrying of firearms.

155

OLD TASCOSA (*above*)

Favorite haunt for off-duty cowboys, old Tascosa reluctantly came under the domination of the powerful XIT. Tascosa lay in a shady cottonwood grove on the Canadian River, and during roundup seasons it became a little "Dodge City."

Here are shown a group of LS cowboys riding into town for a thirst quencher at one of the many bars.

HITCHING RACK IN TASCOSA (*below*)

LS and L I T punchers at hitching rack in front of 'dobe walled saloon in Tascosa.

TASCOSA BAR (*above*)

This cosy bar in Mike's Place was known to many a great name of the Old West. But the coming of the XIT and its fences had doomed the colorful trading town.

ROUNDUP WAGONS IN CLAYTON, NEW MEXICO (*below*)

For a short time, Clayton, New Mexico, just west of the Texas line, served as a trail driving point on the new Denver & Fort Worth Railroad.

157

DODGE CITY COWBOY BAND

Meanwhile, Dodge City had grown prosperous catering to the Texans, prosperous and perhaps "dandified" as some of the old-timers charged. A fancy cowboy band was organized to play for the cattlemen's conventions. The band toured in the east, marching in President Benjamin Harrison's inaugural parade.

JACK RABBIT ROUNDUP (*on facing page, top*)

Symptoms of the great cow town's waning glory were already apparent. Land office business was booming. The "fool hoe men" were on every side. And instead of herding cattle, these new settlers were rounding up jack rabbits!

CATTLEMEN IN ST. LOUIS (*on facing page*)

In 1884, the cattlemen gathered in St. Louis to demand a National Livestock Trail, established by law, extending from Red River in Texas to the Canadian border. But the National Trail died in St. Louis. The day of the trail driver was coming to an end.

159

SHIPPING BUFFALO BONES (*above*)

With the closing of the trails, Dodge City's golden splendor declined rapidly. Founded on buffalo hides, Dodge's glory ended on the stacks of bleaching buffalo bones, considered worthless a few years earlier.

CATTLE ON NORTHWEST RANGE

The last great trail drives were not drives to markets, but were emigrations from a closed range to the last great open range in the United States. Thousands of cattle moved north to flood the grasslands of Wyoming and Montana.

CHAPTER SIX

Billy the Kid

Before the open range cattlemen made their last stand in the northwest, a classic tragedy played out its action on the dry ranges of New Mexico, creating an immortal American legend. Chief actor in this drama was William H. Bonney, better known as Billy the Kid.

The story of Billy the Kid and the Lincoln County War begins properly with John Simpson Chisum, feudal lord of the Bosque Grande, a range one hundred and fifty miles long with a hundred thousand cattle carrying his Long Rail brand and Jingle Bob ear mark. John Chisum was the King of the Pecos. Beside a gushing spring of clear sparkling water, he built a magnificent ranch house, a rambling Spanish adobe with verandas, surrounded by irrigated fields of green alfalfa, blooming fruit trees and towering cottonwoods —all watered by this priceless spring in the heart of a desert.

Chisum was a veteran of the cattle country. During the Civil War, he had made drives to Shreveport on Red River, and after the war he ventured into a packing business in Fort Smith, Arkansas. He formed a business association with Charles Goodnight, while the latter was driving Longhorns on the Goodnight-Loving Trail.

Gradually Chisum built up his empire, and then brought his brothers, Jess, Pittser and James, from Texas to help run the vast range operation. In 1875, brother James's daughter, Sallie Chisum, came to manage the busy household of the Jingle-Bob Ranch.

"I knew Billy the Kid during the Lincoln County War," she said years later, after she married her uncle's bookkeeper, William Robert, and became Sallie Chisum Robert. The Kid and his followers had taken refuge on the Jingle-Bob during the bloody fighting of July, 1878. "Look out, Miss Sallie, take cover!" the Kid shouted. A bullet just missed her head, drilling a hole through a wash pot in which she was doing her laundry.

In the late Seventies, John Chisum's troubles began multiplying as rapidly as his cattle were increasing in numbers. Rustlers raided his far-flung herds. And as more settlers came

161

into New Mexico, the Long Rail and Jingle Bob became the target of land-hungry owners of small ranches on its borders.

In 1875 a former army officer, Major L. G. Murphy, established a general store in Lincoln, the trading center for the ranching country. Murphy became leader of the anti-Chisum forces. In a short time he was also operating a flour mill and hotel, and most important of all—a small ranch adjacent to Chisum's.

The Long Rail cowboys were alert. When they suspected Murphy's riders of rustling their cattle, they passed the word along to John Chisum, who went directly to Lincoln and accused Murphy of planning the thievery. Instead of drawing his gun, Murphy laughed at Chisum. After all, he controlled the town of Lincoln, he had elected the Lincoln County sheriff, and for legal insurance he had just retained a brilliant young lawyer, Alexander McSween.

Young Alexander McSween and his wife had recently arrived in Lincoln from Atchison, Kansas. He was a religious man who always carried a Bible in his saddlebags, and was probably the only adult male in the county who did not pack a gun. With Major Murphy as his client, McSween was soon prospering.

When John Chisum caught some rustlers red-handed on his range and brought them into Lincoln for trial, Murphy called on McSween to defend them. The mild-mannered lawyer investigated the circumstances, then refused politely but firmly to have anything to do with the defense. Naturally, he lost his lucrative job as Murphy's attorney, at the same time arousing the bitter enmity of the major.

Murphy's anger turned to rage when John Chisum soon afterwards retained the honest little lawyer to handle his side of the case.

Into this turbulent setting now came an energetic British character, John H. Tunstall, wearing fancy riding breeches and a checked sporting cap. "The belted earl," the cowboys called him, after his English hunting jacket. Tunstall was fascinated by the New Mexico ranching country, and immediately purchased a spread about thirty miles from Lincoln on the Rio Feliz. He and Alexander McSween soon became close friends.

The two men pooled their resources and built a rival trading store in Lincoln, and they were soon making heavy inroads on Murphy's business. When John Chisum established a bank in the McSween-Tunstall building, Major Murphy knew he would soon have to fight to hold his power in Lincoln County.

Bitterness increased even more when the major accused McSween and Tunstall of embezzling an estate involving a former partner of Murphy. Murphy claimed that the assets of the estate were legally his, and threatened to seize the partners' personal property if they did not turn the money over to him. When McSween and Tunstall refused to budge, Murphy decided to take direct action. Through the sheriff's office, which he controlled, Murphy finally sent twenty armed deputies riding one morning in February, 1878, with orders to take possession of the cattle on Tunstall's ranch.

On this day, young William H. Bonney, the Kid, rode headlong into the dispute to begin a period of bloody action that would end his life and at the same time bring into being the cattle country's most romantic legend.

BILLY THE KID

Billy the Kid began his short life in New York City, on the Bowery in 1859, his parents moving west during the Civil War into the violence of border-state Kansas. After his father died in Coffeyville, his mother went to Colorado, there marrying a man named Antrim. They followed the mining camps into New Mexico.

According to the legend, Billy killed his first man at the age of twelve:

When Billy the Kid was a very young lad
In old Silver City he went to the bad;
Way out in the West with a gun in his hand
At the age of twelve years he killed his first man.

A Silver City blacksmith is said to have made a slighting remark about the boy's mother, and Billy killed the man with a knife. After bidding his mother goodbye, he fled to Arizona, drifting into Fort Bowie, where he lived by doing odd jobs around the post. He also became adept at the art of gambling.

Blacksmiths seemed to fare badly at the hands of the Kid. Pat Garrett, who later killed Billy, says that the boy's second victim was a soldier blacksmith at Fort Bowie. This blacksmith was trying to cheat him in a card game.

Fleeing with a gun-packing partner named Jesse Evans, Billy went south into Mexico, and for several months the two lived by their wits and by their guns. They worked out a system of stealing from Mexicans and fleeing north to safety in New Mexico. Then they would rustle a few cattle from the New Mexican ranchers and jump the border back into Chihuahua.

In the autumn of 1877, as the feud between the McSween-Tunstall-Chisum alliance and the Murphy partisans began to wax hot, Billy the Kid rode into the Pecos valley. He was weary of running back and forth across the border, and was looking for a place to settle down for the winter. Just how he met the Englishman, John Tunstall, is not clear, but it is evident from what followed that Tunstall liked the eighteen-year-old Billy. He gave him a job on his ranch, treated him kindly, and quickly won a loyal friend.

On the chill February morning when Murphy's hired posse swept into Tunstall's ranch and began rounding up the Englishman's cattle, Billy the Kid appears to have been absent from the ranch house. Several versions of the death of Tunstall exist: his men may have deserted him; he may have fired first as Murphy's deputies claimed; or he may have been shot in the back as Pat Garrett later declared.

At any rate, Billy learned of his friend's death before nightfall. In a cold rage he rode into Lincoln to inform Alexander McSween. The lawyer immediately sent some Mexicans out to the ranch, and at dawn they returned to the front of McSween's store with Tunstall's body strapped to a burro.

While Tunstall was being buried, Billy is said to have stood by the grave, clenching his fists and swearing an oath of vengeance: "I'll shoot down like a dog every man who had a hand in this murder."

By noon that day, Lincoln County became a potential battleground. Fifty cattlemen

163

rode in from far distant ranches to rally around McSween. The bold act of the Murphy faction had crystallized them into forming an alliance. They feared that what had happened to Tunstall might happen to them. Meanwhile, Murphy was supported by several of the small ranch owners, by his political henchmen, and undoubtedly by a sizable group of hired gunmen. A small war was in the making.

Violent action followed swiftly. As Murphy controlled the sheriff's office, McSween and the cattlemen decided to elect Tunstall's foreman, Dick Brewer, a special constable, empowering him to raise a posse to search out and arrest Tunstall's murderers. Billy the Kid of course joined the posse. They captured two of the Murphy men, holding them at the Chisum ranch overnight. On the way back to Lincoln for trial, the two men were killed while attempting to escape. Just how hard they tried to escape will never be known, but they were both shot by Billy the Kid.

On April 1, for a grim Fool's Day trick, Billy got two more of Tunstall's enemies. He hid out behind an adobe wall in Lincoln until four of Murphy's men strolled into his gunsights. One of them was Murphy's sheriff, William Brady. The Kid took him with his first shot, and then killed one of the remaining three while they were running for cover. Two weeks later, the Murphy forces struck back. Buckshot Roberts, a Murphy gunman, killed McSween's constable, Dick Brewer. Roberts died in the duel, but McSween had to find another posse leader. The job went to Billy the Kid.

Through the summer of 1878, the war continued. A bloody fight broke out in Lincoln in July, almost at the moment a small Murphy army was trying to smoke Alexander McSween and Billy the Kid out of John Chisum's South Springs ranch house. Chisum's cowboys rode in from a distant roundup just in time to break up the seige, and when the Kid heard what was happening in Lincoln he led his posse into town. But they were too late to join in the battle. He and his men barricaded themselves in McSween's big twelve-room house to wait for morning.

At dawn the Murphy forces had the McSween house surrounded, but before an attack could be launched, McSween arrived with thirty-five men to rescue Billy. A few shots were exchanged, then McSween begged for a parley. He wanted to settle the war before any more blood was shed.

McSween got nowhere with his pleas for peace. Shooting broke out again, and the lawyer's house became a fortress. Although there were few casualties, the battle raged for three days. On the evening of the third day, a distant bugle call cut across the rattle of gunfire.

Echoes of the Lincoln County War had finally reached Fort Stanton, and Colonel Nathan A. M. Dudley came riding into town with a company of infantry, a troop of cavalry, a Gatling gun, and a twelve-pounder cannon. Ignoring the combatants, he drew his soldiers up in front of the McSween residence. Both sides ceased firing, and except for the clinking of harness chains and the snorting of the sweated horses, the town was silent after its three days of gunfire.

In his loudest parade-ground voice, Colonel Dudley shouted toward the house: "Mister McSween!"

McSween stepped out in full view of fifty men who would have shot him dead instantly had the cavalrymen not been there. "This fighting must stop at once," the colonel told McSween.

"I have tried to stop it," replied McSween, "but with no effect."

"You can cease your fire."

"The besiegers started this fight," answered the lawyer. "I am being attacked in my own home. My friends and I are fighting for our lives."

The colonel then explained that he could offer no protection to McSween and his men. Murphy's new sheriff, George Peppin, who was leading the attack, had been legally appointed. In the eyes of the army, McSween was outside the law.

"My orders to you," concluded Colonel Dudley tersely, "are to cease firing. If you do not do so, you must suffer the consequences. My troops cannot interfere with the law."

While this conversation was taking place, some of the Murphy men had crept to the rear of the McSween home and set fire to the back porch. By the time Colonel Dudley had moved his troops away, the back room was blazing.

In a vain attempt to stop the flames, the trapped men used their two barrels of drinking water. But the fire had gained too much headway; the walls and roof of the back room were already collapsing.

Darkness was falling as the flames licked into the center of the big twelve-room house. Two men tried an escape. They were dead before they hit the front steps.

McSween decided to surrender himself to the besiegers, hoping that such an act might save the lives of his friends. Taking his Bible in his right hand, he held it up like a talisman of peace. He stepped outside the front door, the bright flames behind him silhouetting his figure for the waiting gunmen. "Here I am, gentlemen," he called. "I am McSween!" A dozen rifles cracked, and Alexander McSween was dead on the ground.

One by one, the others began dashing out of doors and windows, running madly for the protecting cover of darkness. The roof of the McSween home became a solid mass of orange flame.

Billy the Kid was the last to depart. He loaded and cocked both pistols, noting carefully the positions of the dead lying on the porch, calculating the distance from the door to the back wall of the yard, and then charged out through a choking cloud of smoke.

His pistols were firing continuously. "Here comes the Kid!" somebody yelled, and he was gone, over the wall in one leap and down into the dark brush-grown canyon and the safety of the hills beyond.

The Lincoln County War was now officially ended. McSween was dead. Major L. G. Murphy also was dead, peacefully in bed in Santa Fe where he had gone for medical care shortly before the three-day battle began. With Murphy gone, John Chisum no longer had any interest in the feud. But to Billy the Kid, after the disastrous fight in the burning home of his friend McSween, the score seemed more uneven than ever. He became an avenging spirit, attracting supporters almost as deadly as himself. He determined to search out and destroy every man who had taken part in the siege of the McSween home.

Billy the Kid's private war spread to the cattle ranges. Lonely line riders were dry-gulched, and rustlers were killed in return. The ranch owners, still distrusting the local government, finally called on President Rutherford B. Hayes in Washington to stop the bloodshed. Hayes responded by appointing a new territorial governor in August, 1878. The new governor was General Lew Wallace, soldier and novelist.

With the same thoroughness that he was then devoting to the writing of his novel, *Ben Hur,* Lew Wallace applied himself to studying what he termed the "Lincoln County Insurrection." He took statements from McSween's widow, from Sheriff Peppin, and called in John Chisum for an interview. Finally he decided to have a talk with Billy the Kid, and announced publicly that he would be in Lincoln at a certain time and would grant the young outlaw immunity if he would come in to see him.

Billy the Kid arrived in Lincoln on the governor's appointed hour, packing a rifle across his saddle and a forty-four in his belt. He had dressed for the occasion, wearing a new hat and a fresh bandanna. He stared calmly at Wallace's pince-nez glasses, neat gray mustache and pointed beard.

"So you are Billy the Kid," said Wallace.

"I am," replied Billy, and they shook hands.

They talked for several minutes, the governor attempting to persuade the outlaw either to give up his arms or to leave New Mexico Territory.

"If I walked through Lincoln without my guns," said the Kid, "I'd be killed so quick I wouldn't know what happened to me. And I'm not leaving. This is my country and I'm staying here."

For all Wallace's efforts, the feud continued. To end it, a tall, soft-drawling buffalo hunter from Texas, Pat Garrett, was named sheriff. Garrett had known Billy in Texas and had always liked him, but he realized as well as the governor that the time had come to stop the killings. The Kid had already slain nineteen men.

Garrett selected a posse of the best deputies in the southwest, and for months he tracked the Kid like a bloodhound. Finally Billy was cornered in an abandoned stone hut near Stinking Spring. A gun battle followed, but the Kid surrendered and was taken into Mesilla for trial.

His fate was sealed in the grim faces of the jurors. The judge received the verdict, and began intoning the ritual of the sentence: "You are sentenced to be hanged by the neck until you are dead, dead, dead."

The Kid gave the judge one of his impudent cherubic grins, and replied in a high piping voice: "And you can go to hell, hell, hell."

Under heavy guard he was taken to Lincoln and locked in a room above the late Major Murphy's old general store. Taking no chances, Pat Garrett kept him in handcuffs and leg irons.

But on the very day that Garrett left town to arrange the final details of the hanging, Billy made his escape. He persuaded one of the deputies, Johnny Bell, to play a game of monte with him. During the game he pretended to drop a card, leaned forward as if to pick it up from the floor, grabbed Bell's pistol instead, and shot the deputy dead. Crawling to the window, he saw the other guard, Bob Ollinger, running forward across the street.

166

The Kid fired, and Ollinger was dead before he reached cover. The Kid then forced a terrified jail cook to loose the chain binding his leg irons, stole a horse from the county clerk, and rode out of Lincoln at an easy gallop. He had killed his twenty-first and last man on an April evening in 1881.

Once more Pat Garrett took up the chase. He gathered a new posse, and sent riders off to every town in the area to organize other local posses. Eight weeks passed before Garrett smelled out his quarry near Fort Sumner, where Billy had gone to see the "only girl he ever loved."

Garrett set his trap, waiting in the darkness of a bedroom. The Kid stepped inside the doorway, halting quickly as he sensed some one's presence. *"Quien es?"* he whispered.

"He raised his pistol quickly," Garrett says in his account of the final scene. "Retreating rapidly across the room he repeated: *'Quien es? Quien es?'* All this occurred in a moment. Quickly as possible I drew my revolver and fired, threw my body aside, and fired again. The second shot was useless. The Kid fell dead. He never spoke. A struggle or two, a little strangling sound as he gasped for breath and the Kid was with his many victims."

The day was July 14, 1881.

Six weeks later *The True Life of Billy the Kid* was being sold on the streets of New York. The legend was on its way.

JOHN SIMPSON CHISUM

The story of Billy the Kid and the Lincoln County War begins with John Simpson Chisum, feudal lord of the Pecos, and owner of a hundred thousand cattle branded with the Long Rail and Jingle Bob.

SOUTH SPRINGS RANCH

In the heart of New Mexico's dry range country, John Chisum found an everlasting spring of pure water, and here he built a magnificent ranch house, surrounded by irrigated fields of green alfalfa, blooming fruit trees, and towering cottonwoods.

MAJOR L. G. MURPHY AND FRIENDS (*above*)

Major L. G. Murphy was the leader of political forces opposed to John Chisum's cattle empire. Murphy owned most of the town of Lincoln, and controlled the county sheriff. (*Above, left to right:* J. G. Dolan, Emil Fritz, W. J. Martin, and Major Murphy.)

QUEEN OF THE JINGLE BOB (*on facing page*)

In 1875, John Chisum's niece, Sallie Chisum, came from Texas to manage the busy household. The cowboys soon named her "Queen of the Jingle Bob."

ALEXANDER McSWEEN
AND
JOHN H. TUNSTALL

Alexander McSween and John Tunstall were bitter enemies of Major Murphy. McSween was John Chisum's lawyer, and Tunstall was a neighboring rancher, a Britisher who startled the cowboys by wearing fancy riding breeches and a checked sporting cap.

McSWEEN-TUNSTALL STORE

Pooling their resources, McSween and Tunstall built a new general store in Lincoln, and were soon making sharp inroads into Murphy's lucrative trading monopoly. John Chisum joined the partners by establishing a bank in their building, and Major Murphy soon realized he would have to fight to hold his power in Lincoln County.

BILLY THE KID

As the quarrel between Major Murphy and the Chisum-McSween-Tunstall forces reached the point of violence, young William H. Bonney, the Kid, came upon the scene.

COWBOYS IN BILLY THE KID'S COUNTRY

The Kid never claimed to be a cowboy, but by 1878 he had trailed so many stolen steers over rough southwestern trails that he probably felt he could qualify as an accomplished range hand. Just how he met John H. Tunstall is not clear, but the Englishman gave him a job on his ranch, treated him kindly, and quickly won a loyal friend.

THE KID'S PORTRAIT

Billy was absent the morning that Major Murphy's deputies raided the Tunstall ranch and shot the Englishman to death. But as soon as the Kid heard the news, he rode into Lincoln to inform McSween. The two swore vengeance against Tunstall's killers.

This tintype portrait of Billy the Kid was discovered recently by Rodger de Lashmutt of Glencullen, Oregon, in a family album that belonged to his rancher grandfather. For many years it was believed even by the Kid's biographers that no face and shoulder portrait of him existed.

THE CAVALRY ENTERS THE WAR

Violent action followed swiftly, developing into the Lincoln County War. Finally the United States Cavalry intervened much as in the picture *above,* riding into Lincoln while the Murphy forces were beseiging Billy the Kid and McSween in the lawyer's twelve-room house.

COLONEL NATHAN A. M. DUDLEY

Colonel Nathan Dudley drew his troops up between the combatants, ordering McSween to halt the fighting. McSween agreed to attempt a truce, and the cavalry withdrew. But when the Murphy forces set fire to McSween's house, the lawyer was shot to death. Billy the Kid escaped, swearing to kill every man who had taken part in the siege.

PAT GARRETT (*on facing page*)

To end the feud, a tall buffalo hunter from Texas, Patrick F. Garrett, was named sheriff. Garrett had known Billy in Texas and had always liked him, but the time had come to stop the killings.

177

REWARD

($5,000.00)

Reward for the capture, dead or alive, of one Wm. Wright, better known as

"BILLY THE KID"

Age, 18. Height, 5 feet, 3 inches. Weight, 125 lbs. Light hair, blue eyes and even features. He is the leader of the worst band of desperadoes the Territory has ever had to deal with. The above reward will be paid for his capture or positive proof of his death.

JIM DALTON, Sheriff.

DEAD OR ALIVE!
"BILLY THE KID"

THE LEGEND BEGINS

Pat Garrett captured Billy, but he escaped. The second pursuit ended in the Kid's death, July 14, 1881. Six weeks later, *The True Life of Billy the Kid* was being sold on the streets of New York. The legend was on its way.

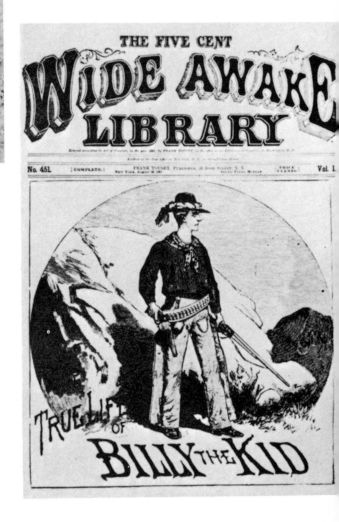

THE LEGEND GROWS

Successors to Billy the Kid were soon appearing among the reward posters in sheriff's offices of the southwest. Billy may have been only a part-time cowboy, but folklore has made him the foremost range-riding Robin Hood of the American West.

CHAPTER SEVEN

Free Grass in the Northwest

Whie Billy the Kid was riding to his doom in the cattle country of New Mexico, the Indians and their buffalo were being swept from the ranges of Wyoming and Montana, and the sacred hunting grounds were filling rapidly with herds of cattle.

The first overland drive from the Texas cattle country to Montana had come as early as 1866, but after that single venture a number of years passed before Texas cattle again crossed the waters of the Yellowstone.

Hero of the 1866 drive was Nelson Story. His journey, while not as long in distance as Tom Ponting's eastern drive of 1852, was all overland, and was certainly more fraught with perils, suspense, and high drama.

Nelson Story, born in Ohio in 1838, had gone west to Denver during the Pike's Peak gold rush. When the Colorado boom collapsed, he moved on to Alder Gulch, Montana, and finally struck pay dirt to the amount of $30,000. By this time, Story was weary of washing gold, and after converting his diggings into greenbacks, he sewed ten thousand dollars into the linings of his clothes and went south to Texas. He believed the cattle business might be just as profitable and probably more interesting than searching for the elusive yellow metal.

Arriving in Fort Worth, he sank most of his ten thousand dollars in a herd of about one thousand Longhorns, hired a crew of cowboys, and in 1866 became one of that army of hopefuls moving north toward the Baxter Springs barricade. Instead of digging in and battling the Jayhawkers, Story detoured. He remembered how hungry he had been for beef when he was digging gold in Montana, and he was certain he could obtain premium prices for every steer he could deliver to the northwestern mining camps. He also must have known it was a foolhardy chance he was taking, but he went boldly ahead with his plans.

At Fort Leavenworth he made thorough preparations for the drive, buying an ox-drawn wagon train and loading it with groceries. His little army of cowboys and bull-

179

whackers moved leisurely along the old Oregon Trail across Kansas and Nebraska to Fort Laramie. At Laramie, the army officers tried to persuade him to abandon his plans for going on to Montana. The Sioux and Cheyenne were swarming all over central Wyoming, attacking everything that moved along the Bozeman Trail. Efforts of the army to keep the trail open by building three forts had served only to arouse the tribes and to weld them into a single fighting force led by a wily leader, Chief Red Cloud.

"Red Cloud will stampede all your cattle and probably take your scalps, to boot," the Laramie officers informed Nelson Story.

Story calmly inspected his twenty-seven cowboys and bullwhackers, examined their arms and ammunition, equipped each man with one of the new Remington rapid-fire breechloaders, and started north.

Near Fort Reno, they met their first Sioux, a war party that boiled up suddenly over a hill. The Indians' hit-and-run punch left two trail drivers badly hurt with arrows. They also cut away a good slice of the herd, leaving the remainder of the Longhorns in a state of stampede.

As soon as Nelson Story and his men had quieted the cattle and taken care of the wounded, they organized a war party of their own to pursue the raiding Sioux. Dusk was falling rapidly, but just before darkness ended the chase, Story and his seasoned trail men tracked the Sioux into their camp. The Indians had the Longhorns bedded down in the center of an arc of teepees.

One of the drivers present on this occasion later said: "We surprised them in their camp and they weren't in shape to protest much against our taking back the cattle." Story also told his son some years afterwards that he had never killed an Indian before that night attack. "We had to wipe out the entire group to recover our Longhorns," he said.

When the herd was reassembled, the drivers pushed them north across Powder River. The summer was waning and Story wanted to move his Longhorns into Montana before snow.

At Fort Phil Kearny where the army was centering its sparse forces for an expected autumn attack from the Sioux, Colonel Henry B. Carrington solemnly advised Story to halt his trail drive if he wished to remain alive. All through the summer, Carrington had been losing men, one or two at a time, and he had acquired a high respect for the cunning of Red Cloud's warriors.

When Nelson Story indicated that he would be moving on north despite the Colonel's warning, Carrington ordered him to halt the herd and wait for permission to leave the vicinity of the fort.

Story was fuming with impatience, but not wishing to tangle with the army, he started his men to building a temporary corral adjoining the fort. Carrington immediately ordered the corral moved three miles from the stockade. When Story pointed out that this distance would give his men and cattle no protection from the fort in case of an attack, Carrington replied that all the grass near the fort was reserved for his cavalry mounts.

For a few hours, Story brooded over this impasse. The date was October 22, and blizzards could be raging in a matter of days. If he intended to act, he must act quickly.

180

That evening, after he heard the bugler blow taps inside the fort, he called his men together.

"If we stay here," he said, "the Indians are going to rush our camp some morning and have us all scalped before the soldiers over at the fort know what's happening. If we go ahead up the trail, they may take our scalps, but I don't think they will. All in favor of moving out tonight say 'Aye.' Opposed say 'No.' "

One driver named George Dow said: "No!"

As soon as the word was out of Dow's mouth, Nelson Story had the man covered with his six-gun. "We'll have to tie you up, George, until we're one day gone."

In the darkness, Story and his men hitched their oxen to the wagons, moved the cattle out of corral, and slipped away north toward Montana. Next day, Dow was released and informed that he could return to Fort Phil Kearny. He decided to stay with the drive.

Later events proved Story had been wise in making his unauthorized departure from the fort. Exactly two months after that October evening, Red Cloud's combined Sioux and Cheyenne warriors wiped out a good part of Colonel Carrington's garrison in the historic Fetterman Massacre.

The trail herd made such good progress on the night it left Fort Phil Kearny that Nelson Story decided to finish the journey by night movements, resting by daylight. Before the herd reached the Yellowstone, the Sioux attacked twice, but only one man was killed. The Remington repeaters which Story had purchased at Fort Laramie were too much for the Indians.

On December 9, 1866, Nelson Story reached Virginia City. Near Livingston, on the Yellowstone, he built a permanent corral, and Montana ranching with Texas cattle was begun.

The drive had been a phenomenal success, but Story had made it just in time. For the next decade, the trail south to Texas was effectively sealed behind him. During that time, northern Wyoming was the battleground for the last great wars of the Indians, culminating in the Custer Massacre on the Little Big Horn; and ending with the capitulation of the chiefs and the retirement of the tribes to the reservations in 1878.

While the wars were being fought to a conclusion, Montana ranching developed slowly, the ranges being stocked with cattle driven eastward from Oregon. The Oregon herds came, of course, from the breeding stock driven west over the Oregon Trail a quarter of a century earlier. Most of the cattle were Durhams, gradually being improved by the introduction of thoroughbred Shorthorn bulls, either brought overland from the east or by boat around Cape Horn.

The great flood of Oregon cattle did not come into Montana and Wyoming until the bonanza years of the Eighteen-eighties. What is probably the earliest diary of a trail drive from Oregon was recorded in 1876 by a seventeen-year-old boy, William Emsley Jackson, who rode that year with a herd from La Grande, Oregon, to Cheyenne, Wyoming. The route followed was to the Fort Hall Indian Agency, southeastward to Bear Lake, then eastward to a point on the Union Pacific Railroad near Granger, on over the Continental Divide at Bridger's Pass, and across Wyoming by way of Rawlins and Laramie to Cheyenne.

Jackson left La Grande on May 23, "to go with Lang and Shadley's cattle to Cheyenne. Overtook the herds on Clover Creek and went driving with Lang's herd May 24, for $30.00 a month."

On June 23 for an unexplained reason he was made cook for the outfit, and when they passed near Shoshone Falls he reports regretfully: "Was within seven miles of the Falls and was greatly disappointed at not getting to see them. The cook could not leave."

Mosquitoes bothered the drivers and the cattle all through the Snake valley. On July 10, two weeks after the Custer Massacre in Montana, they first heard news of that disaster from a party of Oregon-bound emigrants. Jackson immediately became Indian-wary, and the next day after the herd passed through a narrow gap near the American Falls, he commented: "It is said that this was once a favorite place of attack for Indians, and there are about 75 graves there."

On Medicine Bow River they passed a trail herd which had been driven east from Idaho, bound for Laramie. On the Laramie Plain, Jackson stopped his cook wagon at a miners' camp store. "They have for sale a few canned fruits, baking powder, oysters, and some '49' butter, also one jumper, two overshirts, and a pair of overalls, by selling which they seem to expect to get rich, judging from the prices that they ask for them."

Near Laramie, he reported a number of grazing cattle scattered over the plains. It was September now, and all the drivers were complaining of the cold nights. To keep warm they built "rousing old fires" from pitch pine. As they neared Cheyenne, they also complained bitterly of the vast sheep herds which had devoured most of the grass along the route.

At the end of the drive, the Oregon cowboys did not gallop their horses wildly into Cheyenne. Instead they boarded a train at a water-tank stop near the cattle camp, and rode to town in style.

If the Wyoming cow capital of 1876 bore any resemblance to the Kansas trail towns, young William Jackson does not reveal it. "Took a square meal at Ocean Wave restaurant for .25 cents, after which took a shave, a shampoo and a bath, and put on some clean clothes. I left my watch at a jewelers and wandered around through town the balance of the day, looking at the curiosities and works of art. Cheyenne is quite a large flourishing town of probably 8,000 population and is the most convenient shipping point for the Black Hills."

Nine years before William Jackson made his drive from Oregon, cattlemen were establishing ranches in southern Wyoming and in Colorado. As has been recorded in a previous chapter, Oliver Loving and Charles Goodnight drove Longhorns from Texas to Colorado in 1867 and 1868, selling them to John W. Iliff as stocker herds. And Goodnight himself owned for a few years a ranch near Pueblo.

It was John Iliff, however, who became the first "cattle king of the plains." Iliff was an Ohio college man who joined the Colorado gold rush in 1859. He became a trader to the miners, and soon found that the demand for beef in Colorado was much greater than the supply. In a few years he was running herds on practically all the grazing lands in northeastern Colorado. Iliff was one of the first cattlemen to recognize the value of water rights, and by filing strategic claims in the names of all his friends and cowhands, he controlled about a hundred miles along the Platte. Julesburg was Iliff's headquarters. With stocker cattle moved up by the thousands over the Goodnight-Loving Trail, he made a fortune after fattening them on his extensive range by selling the beef to the miners, to workers in railroad camps, and to the government for distribution on the Indian reservations.

Iliff probably never owned more than forty thousand cattle at any one time; he believed in the quick turnover of his stock. John Hittson, a Texan who came to Colorado during this early period, ran his holdings up to one hundred thousand head of cattle. But Hittson suffered continually from wholesale rustling, and once had to lead an expedition into New Mexico to recover thousands of his stolen cattle.

John Iliff was one of the first cattlemen to recognize the possibilities of ranching in Wyoming. He is credited with being the second man—Nelson Story was the first—to trail Texas cattle across the Wyoming border. In February, 1868, he brought a slaughter herd into Cheyenne, sold part of the beef to local merchants, and shipped the remainder already butchered to Chicago.

In October of the same year, the first Wyoming range herd was established outside Fort Laramie. Two Indian traders, W. G. Bullock and B. B. Mills, purchased this herd in Kansas and Missouri. Their experiences set the pattern of Wyoming ranching for a decade. Indians searching vainly for the vanishing buffalo began raiding the ranchers' cattle, forcing them to establish fortified camps. Until the power of the Indians was broken in 1878, all Wyoming ranches operating north of the Union Pacific Railroad had to be built like small forts.

As the years passed and the Indians began to retreat to the north or to the reservations, the cattlemen pressed forward to the Powder River valley and to the basin of the Big Horns. The winter of 1877-78 finally saw the breaking of the dam. By 1879 there were enough ranches along the Powder to organize Johnson County, and thousands of cattle were being trailed into the watered ranges of the Tongue, the Belle Fourche, the Greybull and the Shoshone.

The Beef Bonanza, which has already been described, was developing in Wyoming just as it had in Texas. Most of the ranchers moving into the lush grasslands of the Indians' sacred buffalo country were men of wealth, or were experienced agents employed by financial syndicates.

Several of the larger Texas companies either moved their holdings into Wyoming and Montana, or established subsidiary ranches. The brands of the XIT and the Matador came to be as well known in the Northwest as they had been in the Southwest.

As the bonanza period developed, Wyoming became the mecca for wealthy and adventurous men from all over the world. English and Scottish noblemen, German barons and French counts, Harvard, Yale and Princeton graduates—were riding the ranges with the drawling Texans who also came in large numbers.

It was not unusual to find polo ponies in corrals adjoining cow ponies, and "postage-stamp" English riding saddles hanging next to lariated Spanish saddles. The term "remittance man" came from the practice of ne'er-do-well sons of wealthy Britishers spending all their money and then awaiting remittances from home. Everything was done on a grand scale; they brought valets and chefs; they built expensive ranch houses furnished with imported rugs and chairs; they laid in huge stocks of fine wines and whiskeys. Dress suits were worn to ranch parties, and one of the many stories still told about that period concerns a young British nobleman invited to a Christmas dinner by a neighboring rancher thirty miles away. He went in a dress suit, through a howling blizzard, and on arrival had to be lifted from his horse frozen like a sitting statue.

John Clay, a Scotchman who managed one of the pioneer Wyoming cattle companies, has left a colorful record of these days in *My Life on the Range*. The British companies, he says, "were mostly floated in Scotland and it is simply marvelous how freely the Scottish investors loaded up with securities of this character."

But somehow the routine tasks of raising cattle were performed, the everyday work on the range being quite similar to the pattern set in the Southwest. The clothing and the working gear differed slightly; the terminology of the cowboys sometimes differed considerably. Woolly angora chaps and Cheyenne wing chaps were the fashion in the Northwest. The hats were not only creased differently, they were usually called hats and not sombreros. The Texas "remuda" had become a "cavvy." Chute branding was more frequently used than in Texas. And instead of single ranch roundups, several ranchers would combine operations into a general "pool roundup."

But the line riding, the herding, the cutting out, the river crossings, and the drives to market were performed in the usual manner, requiring plenty of muscle, sweat, and hard skillful riding. The trail drives, of course, were much shorter than the old Texas-to-Kansas drives. The Union Pacific and the Northern Pacific Railroads were only a few days away at the most, and the celebrations at the ends of the drives were mild affairs. In the northwest, the cowhands did most of their town celebrating on customary holidays, such as Christmas and New Year's Day.

By 1880, the Wyoming cattle boom was well under way. Cheyenne, which had become almost a cosmopolitan city, was the center of operations, and the luxurious Cheyenne Club was the headquarters for all the wealthy cattlemen.

The cattlemen's lives fell into a set ritual, geared to spring and autumn roundups. Just before the spring roundups, it was the custom for the ranch owners to gather in Cheyenne for a week of celebrating at the club, then off they rode for a month or so on the ranges. Most of their summers also were spent in Cheyenne, where the club provided practically all the facilities that could be found in any similar London establishment. The management was very proud of the fact that the Cheyenne was the first club in the United States to replace the old gas lamps with electric lights. On its walls hung Albert Bierstadt's "In the Heart of the Big Horns," and a realistic painting of a huge bull by Paul Porter. The latter had been pierced by a bullet from a critical cattleman's six-shooter. As the club frowned on such exhibitions of exuberance, the wounded bull was retired to a back room.

The Cheyenne Club's exterior was not particularly pretentious, but in the summer its broad veranda would be filled with cattlemen in dinner clothes sipping cool drinks from tall glasses, and probably reading the London *Times*.

184

Tennis matches, dances, and banquets filled out the summer season. Then, early in the autumn the cattlemen all disappeared, riding off to their ranches like young medieval knights to lead the roundups. When the cattle counts and the antelope hunts were ended, they came back to Cheyenne, but stopped only briefly this time, just long enough to make arrangements for winter departures to the East, to England, and to the Continent.

The cattle business had come a long way since those first perilous drives from Texas in 1866, across Red River and through the Indian Nations to old Abilene town.

Big-time ranching was also developing rapidly on the western Dakota ranges, where the last dwindling herds of buffalo had retreated to die from the bullets of wealthy sportsmen, who came out on special railroad excursions for the hunts.

A French nobleman, Count Fitz-James, who accompanied one of these hunting parties in 1882, returned to France and related such glowing stories of the Dakota country to his cousin, the Marquis de Mores, that the latter decided to pay a visit to the Bad Lands and see them for himself.

And so one day in April 1883, the private railroad car of Antoine de Vallombrosa, the Marquis de Mores, was shuttled off on a sidetrack in the town of Little Missouri. Railroad men on the Northern Pacific called Little Missouri the "toughest town on the line." But as succeeding events proved, the Marquis was a fair match for any of the gamblers, trappers, buffalo hunters, and cattle rustlers who ruled the dives of Little Missouri.

The Marquis was a dynamic Frenchman, tall, muscular and athletic, with black curly hair and an upturned moustache waxed to needle points. A few months earlier in Cannes, he had met and wedded Medora von Hoffman, daughter of a millionaire New York banker. The dowry was said to have been $3,000,000, and as soon as he saw the miles of unclaimed buffalo grass awaiting herds of cattle, the Marquis was prepared to invest it all in the Bad Lands.

He went into action immediately. He was friendly even to the most hostile of the citizens of Little Missouri, and quickly adopted the dress of the country, wearing the widest hats and the most flamboyant bandannas obtainable. He also adopted western weapons. A newspaper man once met him for an interview and reported: "He was armed to the teeth. A formidable looking belt encircled his waist, in which were stuck a murderous looking knife, a large revolver and two rows of cartridges, while in his hand he carried a repeating rifle."

If the local citizens judged the "crazy Frenchman" to be another foreign tenderfoot, they soon discovered their error. The Marquis had heard of water rights, and by careful placement of claims along the Little Missouri River, he became owner of 45,000 acres which effectively controlled several hundred thousand acres of grazing lands. For this feudal empire, he expended only $32,000. He was soon buying trail herds wholesale, as fast as they could be moved into the Bad Lands.

The Marquis won no local friends by this action, and when he discovered that Little Missouri disapproved of his plans to build a meat-packing plant as an adjunct to his ranch, he decided to create a new town east of the river. The town was named Medora after his wife, and he immediately began construction of a chateau on an elevation overlooking the stream. The chateau was a frame structure of twenty-eight rooms, lavishly furnished with oriental rugs and imported Sheraton furniture. To keep the decorations partly indigenous, he included some hand-hewn cottonwood furniture and a few bearskin rugs.

When his wife arrived to manage the chateau, the town discovered that the Marquise was as dynamic as her husband. The Frenchman's cowboys were soon calling her "the Queen of the Bad Lands." The chateau had a butler, a coachman, a gardener, a laundress, and several chambermaids and cooks.

In Chicago about this time, meat packer Gustavus Franklin Swift was proving that refrigerator cars could be used for shipping meat over long distances. The Marquis became interested when he heard the Chicago packer referred to as "that crazy man Swift who believes he can ship fresh meat to local markets." Swift's plan was to slaughter cattle at their points of origin, and save enough in shipping costs to undersell his competitors. If Swift could do it, reasoned the Marquis, then so could he, "that crazy Frenchman of Medora." He would go even farther and eliminate the meat-packing middleman by selling direct from the range to the consumer.

After convincing his wealthy father-in-law and a few western financiers that his scheme was practical, de Mores organized a $10,000,000 company which he called the Northern Pacific Refrigerator Car Company. Railroad cars using the latest refrigerating equipment were ordered constructed, and through the summer of 1883 trainloads of building materials rolled into Medora. By autumn the Marquis had his packing plant in operation. It had the most modern machinery available, even a new blood-drying machine which cost him ten thousand dollars. He planned to use the fertilizer by-products in growing 50,000 cabbages in individual pots under glass, rushing them to early markets for premium prices.

This was only the beginning. He built a large hotel, the "De Mores," as well as a theater and a clubhouse equipped with billiard tables and bowling alleys for the use of his cowboys and butchers. Just for a hobby, he established a two-hundred-mile stageline to Deadwood. This transportation project finally won him some grudging support from the Bad Lands citizens. To operate the coaches, the Marquis employed the local newspaper editor, A. T. Packard, who was a graduate and star baseball player of the University of Michigan. Young Packard was a comparative newcomer also, but the frank reporting in his newspaper, the *Bad Lands Cowboy,* had won the hearts of his six hundred subscribers in western Dakota.

When de Mores asked Packard to take charge of the line, the newspaper editor protested: "But I never saw a stage or stageline. I don't know anything about stagecoaches." The Marquis replied that he would rather have an honest manager than an experienced one, and Packard accepted the job. Four fancy coaches were ordered, application was made for a mail contract, and fast horses were selected. The coaches were christened "Kittie," "Medora," "Dakota," and "Deadwood," and had "United States Mail" emblazoned upon their sides—although the mail contract was never awarded. Packard succeeded in

186

getting the line into smooth operation, but most of its business was lost in a few months when Deadwood began to decline and rival lines started operations to Miles City. The gaily painted coaches were finally sold to Buffalo Bill Cody who re-christened all four of them "Deadwood," and wore them out, one by one, in his Wild West Show.

Meanwhile, to assure control of all the major western markets for meat, de Mores had begun establishing branch slaughter houses at Miles City and Billings, and took his company right into the center of the big meat-packing competition by building cold storage plants in New York, Chicago, Milwaukee, and other cities.

Just what motivated the Marquis in his grand design is not clear. Legend has it that he was in line for the throne of France and planned to use the wealth gained from his huge cattle operations to finance a revolution and re-establish the monarchy with himself as king.

In the midst of the Frenchman's whirl of activity, violence intruded suddenly when he became involved in a quarrel with three buffalo hunters, Riley Luffsey, Frank O'Donald, and Dutch Wannigan. The disagreement started when de Mores fenced part of his land. In the free range country, fencing of any kind was considered a public offense, a crime almost as heinous as horse stealing. It was a "nester trick," abhorred by both hunters and cattlemen. But the Marquis wanted his breeding herds fenced in, and the wire was strung across an old trail where the hunters were accustomed to trail their pack horses.

A few days after the work was completed, the fence was cut. The Marquis rode out, inspected the damage, and ordered the holes mended. But the wire snippers immediately went to work again. After repairing the damage once more, de Mores set an ambush for the hunters. As soon as they rode up to his fence, he opened fire, and Riley Luffsey was killed, O'Donald and Wannigan wounded. Feeling ran high against the Marquis in the community. He was arrested, jailed, and then released. The trial dragged on for weeks, during which time the Marquis added 12,000 sheep to his range, a move which made him more unpopular than ever among the cattlemen. But he was finally acquitted of the murder charge.

The Marquis's mushrooming empire was beginning to totter even before the Great Blizzard of 1887 practically wiped out his herds. His meat business was running a loss of over a million dollars a year, and his alarmed father-in-law, from whose pockets the money was coming, had journeyed to Medora to advise suspension of operations. The Marquis did not capitulate, however, before announcing through the *Bad Lands Cowboy* one more magnificent scheme for recovering his losses:

> "Marquis de Mores has completed contracts with the French government to supply its soldiers with a newly invented soup. He intends to visit Europe soon to make contracts with western range cattle companies who have their headquarters there, for the slaughtering of their herds."

But in the spring of 1887, the Marquis with his family and entourage boarded his private railroad car in Medora and departed forever. The chateau and its contents were left almost intact—the twenty-eight rooms of costly furniture, the children's toys, and numerous leather trunks packed with the personal belongings of the charming Marquise.

After returning to France, the Marquis became involved in the Alfred Dreyfus affair, went to India to hunt lions, started a railroad in China, and finally was killed in a battle with Arabs in Africa.

Today his chateau still stands in the midst of the Bad Lands, a curiosity for tourists. And facing defiantly down the main street of Medora, the town he built, is a bronze statue of Antoine de Vallombrosa, the Marquis de Mores, dressed in the costume of an American cowboy.

A close neighbor but not a close friend of the Marquis de Mores was another man of action, a young New Yorker who was destined to become one of the United States' most colorful presidents. His name was Theodore Roosevelt. A pale, slender, shy young man in his twenties, Roosevelt arrived in Medora in September, 1883, about the time the Marquis was building his chateau. He came for a short hunting trip, but stayed for four years. During this period he operated two ranches, wrote several books, and developed his philosophy of self-reliance and direct action which carried him to the White House.

Although there was some similarity in the natures and tastes of the dynamic Frenchman and the energetic New Yorker, they exchanged visits only occasionally, and toward the end of the Marquis's dizzy whirl across Dakota, he and Roosevelt almost met in a duel. Roosevelt chose to go his own way in the West. He spent most of his spare time writing hunting books and biographies. He preferred the quiet life of the ranch to the hullabaloo of Medora, and soon found that his rough cowboys could discuss books and politics much more picturesquely and quite as entertainingly as the cultured Frenchman.

Only a few days after Roosevelt's arrival in the Bad Lands, he made up his mind to become a ranch owner. Aware that he knew nothing of the problems involved, he established a partnership with two of his hunting companions, Bill Merrifield and Sylvane Ferris, who already owned a small ranch.

Known as the Maltese Cross, the Roosevelt ranch began operations on a small scale, with about three hundred cattle the first year, increasing to a thousand head in the spring of 1884. As was the practice in the open range country, the partners owned no land, but filed a claim for grazing rights along a section of the Northern Pacific Railroad.

From Sylvane Ferris, Theodore Roosevelt learned how to saddle a cow pony, and in a short time conquered his intense fear of bucking horses. But he was remarkably slow at learning the terminology of the range country. One of the stories told about him during his first year in the Bad Lands concerns a phrase he used in ordering a cowboy to head off a steer. Rising in his stirrups, Roosevelt shouted in his correct Harvard accent: "Hasten forward quickly there!" All the cowhands in hearing distance burst out laughing. They immediately adopted the words as their own, and "Hasten forward quickly there" could be heard ringing on the Maltese range for weeks afterwards.

As were all easterners come to the West, Roosevelt was considered a dude at first; just another tenderfoot. The huge round eyeglasses which he wore soon won him the nickname of "Four Eyes."

188

It was during his second year in the Bad Lands that the nickname was altered. On a bitter cold day, Roosevelt had been trailing some strayed horses, and night fell before he could ride back to the ranch house. Because of the weather, he decided to stop in Mingusville, a railroad station which boasted a single combination hotel and saloon.

As he approached the saloon entrance, two shots suddenly exploded inside. A bearded man, obviously drunk, was shambling up and down the floor, carrying two cocked pistols in his hands. He had just shot two holes in the clock above the bar. Most of the men inside were sheep herders, busily pretending they did not know the gunman existed.

"Four Eyes!" cried the drunk as soon as he saw Roosevelt. "Four Eyes is going to set up drinks!"

Roosevelt calmly ignored him, and moved directly toward the stove to warm his hands. "Four Eyes is going to treat us," the gunman began chanting drunkenly. He waved his guns recklessly toward Roosevelt, becoming more voluble and profane by the second.

Roosevelt was unarmed. He finished warming his hands, turned around slowly, and then suddenly delivered a blow that would have pleasured John L. Sullivan. Both guns roared, but the bullets went wild. The gunman dropped senseless to the floor.

In a matter of hours, news of the affair was all over the Bad Lands. It seemed that everyone who heard it delighted in repeating the story. "Four Eyes" became known affectionately as "Old Four Eyes." Theodore Roosevelt was now "one of the boys."

In a few more months he had become "Mister Roosevelt," and some of the Dakota newspapers began booming him as a possible candidate for Congress. Temporarily, however, Roosevelt had had enough of politics back in New York. He let it be known that while he was in the Bad Lands he was more interested in ranching than in politics.

Selecting an excellent grazing area in the Elkhorn bottoms, he established his second headquarters, the Elkhorn Ranch, and began buying more cattle. Like the Marquis de Mores, he loved the costume of the cowboys. He wore dashing wide-brimmed hats with flat tops, bandannas of fine silk, fringed buckskin shirts, sealskin chaps, and alligator-hide boots. After the affair in the Mingusville saloon, he added two pearl-handled revolvers.

In the spring of 1885, he decided to perfect his knowledge of ranching by participating as an ordinary cowhand in a roundup. He delighted in breakfasting in the cold at three o'clock in the morning, and in riding fifty miles a day. He invented his own lullaby to sing to the cattle when riding night herd. The other cowhands finally forgave him his daily practice of shaving and brushing his teeth. At the end of the roundup, one of them commented: "That four-eyed maverick has got sand in his craw a-plenty."

It was during the time of the Marquis de Mores' legal troubles over the shooting of Riley Luffsey that Roosevelt and the Frenchman almost came to dueling. The indictment of de Mores had been brought about largely through the efforts of Dutch Wannigan, who had been wounded by the Marquis at the time Luffsey was killed. Wannigan was employed on Roosevelt's ranch, and the Frenchman believed that Roosevelt had assisted the cowhand in arranging the murder charge. The Marquis had also been brooding over his meat-packing losses, and he had hinted that Roosevelt might be in league with his enemies, the big packing companies and the railroads.

De Mores finally wrote a threatening letter to Roosevelt, using a phrase intimating that he would like to fight a duel. When Roosevelt replied that he would fight with rifles, the Marquis immediately apologized, claiming he had been misunderstood.

The two men had no more trouble after this. In fact they made their peace and joined forces in one of the northwest's greatest campaigns against stock thieving, a manhunt which originated in the Montana rangelands.

In the early Eighties, Montana ranchers were suffering heavy losses from cattle rustlers and horse thieves. Horse stealing was even worse than cattle rustling, good horses being scarce in the new range country, and for a time they were better legal tender than gold dust. This situation arose when a multitude of whiskey traders swarmed into Montana to sell their potent beverages to the reservation Indians. As the Indians had no money, the liquor traders had to use the barter system, with horses placed high on the list of desirable property for trading. When the Indians had traded in all their own mounts, they began making quick raids on the isolated ranches, chasing off horses faster than the ranchers could replace them. In his diary, Granville Stuart reports a raid in 1881 by Canadian Indians. Twenty-five horses were stolen.

Finally the losses became so severe, the cattlemen requested aid from the military posts in the range country. The cavalrymen went into action, chased down the raiding Indians, and recovered a few horses. Stricter reservation policies were then adopted, and the Indians found it more difficult to get out of bounds.

But as soon as the Indians were under control, gangs of white outlaws began operating on a big scale, rustling cattle and horses together. At the end of one of the bigger pool roundups in western Montana, the ranchers discovered that three thousand of their cattle had been stolen in one season. As a result of this lawlessness, the ranchers organized the Montana Stock Growers' Association to protect their property. They met in Miles City in April, 1883, held a parade, and then settled down to serious business.

Leader of the association was a soft-spoken gentleman from Virginia, Granville Stuart, who had made the first gold strike in Montana in 1858. In the summer of 1879, Stuart organized a cattle ranching firm in Helena, and after several months of touring through the Yellowstone River valley, he selected a range on what had been one of the Indians' choicest hunting grounds, east of the Judith Basin.

Some years earlier, Stuart had helped wipe out organized stagecoach robbers in western Montana, but he hated unnecessary killings. He proposed to employ stock detectives, one for each county in western Montana, use them to gather evidence, and attempt to convict the thieves in the courts. But after a year's trial, he saw that this plan would not stop the rustling. The legal machinery in Montana in those days was ineffectual, and the cattle thieves began scattering their bases of operation, spreading into Wyoming and the Dakotas, making it more difficult than ever to find them and their stolen cattle. In the lawless country of the Bad Lands, the thieves began to fatten off the unprotected herds of such men as the Marquis de Mores and Theodore Roosevelt.

One day in the spring of 1884, Roosevelt and the Marquis boarded a train in

Medora and rode to Miles City to attend the second annual meeting of the Montana Stock Growers' Association. Recognizing that the problem of stock thieving had spread beyond territorial boundaries, Granville Stuart had invited them and several other cattlemen from beyond the Montana line.

The first order of business was a demand that a small army of cowboys be organized to search out the rustlers in their hidden cabins and fight them down in open warfare. Roosevelt and de Mores both joined in this demand, but Stuart and some of the older cattlemen blocked the proposal. Stuart pointed out that the rustlers were well armed, all were desperadoes and dead shots; many cowboys would lose their lives, and those who survived would have to stand trial in the Montana courts for the murder of any rustlers they might kill. Although he did not say so publicly in the stockmen's meeting, the soft-talking Virginian had another plan.

When he returned to his ranch, Stuart found that in his absence the emboldened thieves had stolen his best stallion and thirty-five of his prized steers. As soon as the spring roundup was ended, he called a meeting of fourteen of the most close-mouthed cattlemen in the northwest. They met secretly at his ranch, and called themselves the Vigilance Committee.

In a few weeks they were known as Stuart's Stranglers. The Stranglers worked methodically. When a stock thief became known, he was tracked down, captured, and quietly hanged. A simple placard labeled "Horse Thief" or "Cattle Thief" was always left fastened to each victim's clothes. The northwestern newspapers, aware of what was happening, kept almost as silent as the Stranglers. The *Mineral Argus* of Maiden, Montana, commented laconically: "Eastern Montana is rapidly reducing the number of horse thieves."

The Stranglers became so deadly in their efficiency that on some occasions they permitted the names and dates of the hangings of their next victims to be known in advance. A. T. Packard, editor of the *Bad Lands Cowboy*, once learned that two horse thieves well known in Medora were scheduled to be hanged on a certain Thursday. As that was his press day, he decided to print the news of their executions, being rather confident that the Stranglers would keep their appointed date.

That afternoon as he was putting his mail shipment of the newspaper on the railroad train, the young editor saw the two desperadoes step off the passenger car, very much alive. Packard was more than mildly shocked. He stood there, wondering if the hardened pair intended to stop in Medora, and if so, would they read the current edition of the *Bad Lands Cowboy?* When the train began to move out, the two men stepped back aboard. Packard was immensely relieved. And before the next sunrise, the two horse thieves were dead, as scheduled.

By the autumn of 1884, the Montana and Dakota ranges had been swept clean of stock thieves. No one can say for certain how many men were hanged. Estimates run as high as seventy-five, but hundreds more fled the northwest, a few retreating south to the Hole-in-the-Wall country of Wyoming. A few years later, the ranchers of Wyoming would come to know them as the Hole-in-the-Wall Gang, or the Wild Bunch.

NELSON STORY

Hero of the first overland cattle drive from Texas to Montana was Nelson Story. Following the Bozeman Trail, Story moved a herd of Longhorns across Wyoming in 1866 through thousands of hostile Sioux. At Fort Phil Kearny the army stopped him, forbidding him to proceed any farther. But Story slipped away one night, heading his steers out for the Montana gold fields.

TRAILING INTO MONTANA

The Sioux attacked twice, but early in December 1866, Nelson Story and his drivers and cattle safely reached the Yellowstone. Because of subsequent Indian wars, his was not only the first but was also the last herd of Texas cattle to cross Wyoming for almost a decade.

"A MONTANA RANCH, COMFORTABLE IF NOT ELEGANT"

While the Indian wars were being fought to a conclusion, Montana ranching developed slowly. The ranch houses were scattered widely across the vast Territory. William H. Jackson's note on the above photograph made in 1872: "A Montana ranch, comfortable if not elegant."

WHEN HELENA WAS LAST CHANCE GULCH (on facing page, top)

Montana ranchers found good markets for beef in the goldfield boomtowns such as Last Chance Gulch, which later changed its name to Helena and became the Montana capital.

PIONEER WYOMING RANCH (on facing page)

Cattle ranching in Wyoming developed a few years later than in Montana. The first ranchers were confined to the protected area below the Union Pacific Railroad. During the period of the Indian wars in the north, a number of Oregon trail herds were driven eastward across this section of Wyoming.

195

WILLIAM EMSLEY JACKSON

What is probably the earliest diary of a trail drive from Oregon to Cheyenne was recorded by William Emsley Jackson in 1876. The route followed was from La Grande, Oregon, over the Continental Divide and across Wyoming by way of Rawlins and Laramie to Cheyenne. Near Laramie, Jackson reported seeing a number of grazing cattle scattered over the plains.

CHEYENNE, 1876

If the Wyoming cow capital bore any resemblance to the Kansas trail towns, William Jackson's diary does not reveal it. Instead of galloping their horses into Cheyenne, the Oregon cowboys boarded a train at a water tank stop and rode to town in style.

JOHN WESLEY ILIFF

The first cattle king of the Colorado plains was John Wesley Iliff, who purchased his original stocker herd from Oliver Loving and Charles Goodnight in 1867. Iliff controlled grazing lands along a hundred-mile stretch of the Platte.

COLORADO COWBOYS IN DUGOUT

John Iliff's cowboys lived in dugouts, scattered up and down the Platte. The earthen floors were fine for playing a favorite game, mumble-peg, *as shown below.* Julesburg was head-quarters for Iliff's extensive range operations.

HERD ON POWDER RIVER

As the Indians retreated to the reservations in 1877-78, the cattlemen pushed northward. Texas herds streamed into the coveted grasslands of the Powder River valley. This photograph shows a drive up from the Texas Matador ranch.

XIT IN MONTANA

In a few years, familiar southwestern brands were moving into Wyoming and Montana. The XIT leased two million acres between the Yellowstone and the Missouri, driving herds of ten thousand young steers from the Panhandle to Montana for pasture finishing. Here is a popular XIT cook, Mexican John, baking pies for cowboys during a Montana roundup.

ROPING A MAVERICK

The everyday routines on the northwestern range were quite similar to those developed in the southwest. The clothing, the working gear, and the terminology differed slightly. For instance, the Texas *remuda* had become a *cavvy,* and the hats were not only shaped differently, they were usually called hats and not *sombreros.*

TRAIL BOSS ON NORTHWEST RANGE (*on facing page, top*)

A comparison of this photograph of a northwestern trail boss with the southwestern trail boss on page 43 reveals similarities as well as differences in dress and equipment. Hats are creased differently. The northwestern boss wears woolly chaps, while the southwesterner wears boots only. Both men, however, wear bandannas and opened vests, and the yellow slicker folded behind the saddle of the trail boss was also well known to the Texan.

BRANDING STEERS (*on facing page*)

The XIT influence led to an increase in chute branding, but most ranchers held to the old branding fire and corral system. Contemporary photographs of branding in the northwest usually show the branders with their feet planted solidly on the ground; in the southwest the cowboys apparently preferred to kneel or sit while applying the hot iron.

CHUCK TIME

Chuck was chuck everywhere, under the hot suns of the southwest or in the chill air of the northwestern high plains. But the cozy tents shown above were seldom seen in Texas or New Mexico.

BUNKHOUSE ON HAT CREEK (*on facing page, top*)

In front of this OW bunkhouse on Hat Creek, the foreman, sporting a gold watch chain, stands with some dignity on the right. The customary single fiddler of the old southwest has developed into a five-piece orchestra. And in the center are two men practicing with boxing gloves, unheard of on southwestern ranges, where the cowboys packed sixshooters and left the fisticuffs to the trail town marshals.

CROSSING POWDER RIVER (*on facing page*)

Trail drives to market were much shorter than the old Texas-to-Kansas journeys. Either the Union Pacific or the Northern Pacific was only a few days away at the most. But there were still rivers to be crossed—a task performed in the usual manner, requiring plenty of nerve, muscle, lung power, sweat, and hard skillful riding.

POSING FOR MR. KIRKLAND

The annual or semi-annual trip to Cheyenne was the big event, and a visit to C. D. Kirkland's studio was usually on every cowhand's round of activities. Above photograph, made in 1882, includes Roy Robinson, Shockey Hall, Newt Abbott, Bartlett Richards, William Ashby and John Harris of the Bridle Bit and Circle Block outfits.

THE CHEYENNE CLUB (*on facing page, top*)

In the early 1880's, Cheyenne was coming to be a cosmopolitan center. Headquarters for the wealthy cattlemen was the Cheyenne Club.

HARRY OELRICHS AND FRIENDS (*on facing page*)

Harry Oelrichs, president of the Anglo-American Cattle Company, was one of the leading spirits in the gay social life of Cheyenne. In the photograph Oelrichs is shown with Standing Elk, Running Hog, and Little Wolf.

ROUNDUP

At summer's end, the cattlemen all disappeared from Cheyenne, riding off to their ranches to lead the autumn roundups. When the cattle counts were in, they departed for the East or Europe, and not until the spring roundups would they be seen in Wyoming again.

CATTLE IN DAKOTA (*above and below*)

Meanwhile, big-time ranching was developing rapidly in the Bad Lands of Dakota. By 1880, the Northern Pacific Railroad was moving mile-long trains of cattle cars—Street's Western Stable Car Lines—loaded with beef bound eastward for the meat packing centers.

MARQUIS DE MORES

One day in April 1883, a debonair Frenchman, the Marquis de Mores, arrived in the town of Little Missouri, Dakota Territory. The Marquis was so impressed by ranching possibilities in the Bad Lands that he decided to invest his fortune in cattle raising.

CHATEAU IN THE BAD LANDS

When the citizens of Little Missouri gave him
a cold reception, the Marquis created a new
town nearby, naming it Medora in honor of his
wife. On an elevation overlooking the river, he
constructed a twenty-eight-room chateau.

MEDORA VON HOFFMAN

Medora von Hoffman, the Marquise de Mores,
was as romantic and magnificent as her husband. She installed a butler, a coachman, a
gardner, a laundress, and several chambermaids
and cooks. The Frenchman's cowboys were
soon calling her "the Queen of the Bad Lands."

GUSTAVUS F. SWIFT AND REFRIGERATOR CAR

In Chicago about this time, meat-packer Gustavus Franklin Swift was proving that refrigerated freight cars were practical for shipping fresh meat over long distances. His plan was to slaughter cattle at their points of origin and save enough in shipping costs to undersell his competitors.

"THAT CRAZY FRENCHMAN'S PACKING PLANT"

The energetic Marquis became interested in refrigerator cars, and decided to improve upon Swift's plan by eliminating the meat-packing middleman, selling direct from the range to the consumer. De Mores organized a ten million dollar company, ordered a number of refrigerator cars, and built a packing plant in Medora.

A. T. PACKARD

The Marquis' free spending soon created a boom in Medora. A. T. Packard, a graduate and star baseball player of the University of Michigan, came to town, and started a newspaper, the *Bad Lands Cow Boy*.

THE BAD LANDS COW BOY

Editor Packard's frank method of reporting the news quickly won for him the loyalty of six
hundred subscribers in western Dakota.

DEADWOOD STAGE LINE

When the Marquis de Mores decided to establish a two-hundred-mile stage line to Deadwood, he asked A. T. Packard to manage his new operation.

Four fancy coaches were purchased, and Packard proved to be an excellent transportation manager. But most of the line's business was lost a few months later when Deadwood began to decline and rival lines began operations to Miles City. The gaily painted coaches were finally sold to Buffalo Bill Cody, who wore them out one by one in his Wild West show.

FENCE CUTTERS

In the midst of the Frenchman's whirl of activity violence intruded suddenly when he became involved in a quarrel with three buffalo hunters, Riley Luffsey, Frank O'Donald and Dutch Wannigan. De Mores had fenced his land, and the hunters cut the wire. The photograph above was made in Nebraska, but demonstrates the fine art of fence cutting as practiced in the open range country.

216

DUTCH WANNIGAN (seated) AND FRANK O'DONALD (on facing page)

After repairing his fence the second time, the Marquis set an ambush for the hunters. As soon as the men rode up to the wire, he opened fire. Riley Luffsey was killed, Frank O'Donald and Dutch Wannigan were wounded. Feeling ran high against the Marquis. He was arrested, jailed, and then released. The trial dragged on for weeks, but he was finally acquitted of the murder charge.

DE MORES DEFIANT (above)

The mushrooming empire of the Marquis finally collapsed after the Great Blizzard of 1887 wiped out his herds. He returned to France and never saw Medora again. Today his chateau still stands in the midst of the Bad Lands, a curiosity for tourists. And facing defiantly down the main street of Medora is a bronze statue of the Marquis dressed in the costume of an American cowboy.

THEODORE ROOSEVELT

A close neighbor of the Marquis de Mores was another man of action, Theodore Roosevelt. Young Roosevelt arrived in Medora in September 1883 for a short hunting trip, but he stayed for four years. A few days after his arrival, he made up his mind to become a cattleman.

MALTESE CROSS RANCH (above)

Known as the Maltese Cross, the Roosevelt ranch began operations on a small scale. From one of his partners, Sylvane Ferris, Roosevelt learned how to handle a cow pony, and in a short time conquered his intense fear of bucking horses.

BAD LANDS COW BOY OFFICE (below)

Theodore Roosevelt did not spend much time in Medora, but when he found it necessary to visit the town he always called on Editor A. T. Packard at the *Bad Lands Cow Boy* office. Around a pot-bellied coal stove in this building, young Roosevelt listened and talked, learning the grass-roots politics that would help carry him to the White House a few years later.

MONTANA ROUNDUP (*above*)

In Montana, meanwhile, the ranchers were not finding life as pleasant as were their friends in Wyoming and the Dakotas. After every roundup, the cattlemen counted heavy losses from rustlers and Indian raiders.

MONTANA BRANDING PEN (*below*)

Brand blotching was common in Montana, and intricate designs were invented to circumvent the thieves.

HORSES WERE LEGAL TENDER

Horse stealing became even worse than cattle rustling, good horses being scarce in the new range country, and for a time they were better legal tender than gold dust.

GRANVILLE STUART

To protect their stock, Montana ranchers organized a Vigilance Committee in 1884. Among the leaders was Granville Stuart, a soft-spoken Virginia gentleman and one of Montana's pioneer cattlemen.

3-William Carver 4-Harvey Logan
2-Harry Longabaugh 1-Ben Kilpatrick 5-Butch Cassidy

THE HANGING TREE (*on facing page*)

Granville Stuart had helped wipe out organized robbery in the goldfields around Helena. He hated unnecessary killings, but he was convinced that his Vigilance Committee's methods were justified in a lawless territory. From trees such as this one near Helena, the rustlers were left dangling, a simple placard labeled "Horse Thief" or "Cattle Thief" fastened to each victim's clothing.

HOLE-IN-THE-WALL GANG (*above*)

By the autumn of 1884, the Montana and Dakota ranges had been swept clean of stock thieves. Many were hanged, hundreds fled the country, and a few retreated south to the Hole-in-the-Wall section of Wyoming. A few years later, the Wyoming ranchers would know them as the Hole-in-the-Wall Gang, or the Wild Bunch.

CHAPTER EIGHT

Big Blizzards and Little Wars

At summer's end of the year 1886, a soft blue haze spread over most of the range country. It had been a dry season; the smokes of many grass fires lay over the land from the Yellowstone valley to the Big Horns and across the Colorado high plains, eastward down the Platte and south to Dodge City. Over the Texas Panhandle and New Mexico's Llano Estacado, the golden sun burned hot into October. Except for the chill nights, dry warm temperatures kept the cowboys in their shirt sleeves, and autumn came to Indian Summer with no break of frost.

In Cheyenne, the northwestern cattlemen were boarding trains for New York, Boston, and New Orleans. They were gayer than ever. Big ranches and little ranches showed good profits, not the one-hundred-per-cent profit of the early bonanza days, but money was plentiful enough. The beef market had sagged a little, but almost everyone had added more cattle to cover the price drops, and the grass was still free. The winter of 1885-86 had been a bad one; the range was dryer than it should be for top-weight steers. But every year could not be a perfect year. Some of the older cattlemen were making worried talk about overstocking the ranges, but there was still plenty of grassland unclaimed.

The weather was too fine for a man to worry—the days sun-drenched, the air pure and crisp and tangy against the colorful splendor of autumn in the West.

But along the upper branches of the Missouri River in Montana, the wild geese and ducks and the song birds were starting south earlier than usual. For the first time since ranching had started in Montana, white Arctic owls appeared on the ranges. When the older Indians saw these strange white birds, they drew their blankets closer and shivered, remembering a winter many moons gone.

The muskrats were building their houses taller and thicker along the creeks; the beavers were working day and night cutting willow brush. In late October the blue haze lifted to high altitudes, creating by day a subdued and unnatural light and by night a ghostly moonlight. The air was dead and still.

Fires burned so much grass on the Montana ranges that Conrad Kohrs prepared to move his Tongue River herds across the line into Canada. Drouths in Wyoming's Powder River valley brought herds north into Montana, and these in turned moved across the Canadian border.

On November 16, the thermometer fell below zero over the Rockies; a northwest wind broke the long silence of the earth and sky, drifting six inches of fine hard snow across the dry ranges. Native stock stood the storm well, but cattle recently brought up from Texas wandered aimlessly in circles.

Three weeks later, a second blizzard was howling across the Yellowstone country. Stagecoach travel was halted for three days. Then the sun reappeared; Christmas was bright and cheery. The cattlemen who had stayed on their ranches for the winter were optimistic over their New Year's toddies.

But now it was January, the Moon of Cold-Exploding-Trees. For sixteen hours on the ninth day of January, a north wind spewed out an inch of snow an hour; the storm continued for ten days. By January 15, the thermometer was forty-six below zero, and the world was white.

On January 28, the Great Blizzard struck the northwest. For seventy-two hours, it seemed as if all the world's ice from time's beginnings had come on a wind that howled and screamed with the fury of demons. It was a tornado of white frozen dust. When the storm ended, millions of open range cattle were scattered for miles, dead or dying, heaped against the barbed wire fences of homesteaders, frozen stiff as statues in solid drifts, drowned in the air pockets of snow-blanketed rivers. The gulches and the coulees were filled with snow to depths of a hundred feet or more, leveling with the land. Ranch houses were completely drifted over.

The cowboys stumbled through snow up to their shoulders, rode floundering cow ponies to drifts where they dug out surviving steers. The men wore all the clothing they could fasten around their bodies; they blacked their faces with burned matches to fight the snow glare; but many a cowboy died in the aftermath of the Great Blizzard.

In Great Falls, Montana, five thousand hunger-mad cattle stormed into the streets, uprooted hundreds of recently planted trees to devour the branches and roots; then they fought each other for bits of garbage thrown into the snow. Eastward in Dakota, hundreds of gaunt and bony steers drifted into Medora, eating tar paper from the sides of the shacks until they dropped and died. Wolves and coyotes roamed the frozen range in packs, howling until their bellies were filled from the easy kills.

On February 11, the Bismarck *County Settler* reported "an appalling loss of human lives in Montana and Western Dakota." Whole families were found frozen to death in their thin-walled cabins; those in dugouts fared better.

On Wyoming's plains the great herds of the cattle syndicates searched desperately for shelter in canyons and under rimrocks, but thousands drifted against homesteaders' fences and died there in frozen masses. The survivors had a chance until a chinook blew warm and melting for one day early in February, then vanished before an Arctic blast that froze the melted snow into an impenetrable sheet over the precious grass.

In western Kansas, five thousand of a herd of fifty-five hundred cattle died in the storm. The Dodge City *Daily Globe* reported in January: "Within a few miles of here, no less than five hundred cattle have drifted to the river, where they perished in attempting to cross, or drifted up to fences, where they remained until frozen to death. A gentleman from a ranch south of here reports seeing cattle on his way up that were still standing on their feet frozen to death."

Finally in March the sun burned through the cold gray haze. For the first time in weeks over the northwest ranges, the sky was blue again. A chinook poured warmth down over the mountains, and trickles of melted ice flowed down the slopes, uncovering the brown grass. In a few days the Little Missouri was in flood, rushing out of its banks, its huge ice cakes smashing tall trees in the bottom lands. The river was filled with the frozen carcasses of cattle, rolling over and over in the churning current, bobbing up and down on the crests of the flood waters.

As the snow retreated, the cattlemen could count their losses. Coulees and wooded areas were packed with dead cattle; occasionally a grotesquely frozen steer was found high in a tree's crotch, where it had struggled over drifts to gnaw at the bark and then die.

In Montana, Granville Stuart rode over his range and decided he wanted no more of the cattle business: "I never wanted to own again an animal that I couldn't feed or shelter."

Not until they held their spring roundups did the cattlemen know the real truth, and then "it was only mentioned in a whisper." The roundups were dismal affairs, no joking, no singing, not much talk. No one could take pleasure in cutting out and roping the gaunt survivors of what had once been the greatest range herds in the world.

Through the spring and summer one after another of the great cattle firms closed out or went bankrupt. "From southern Colorado to the Canadian line, from the 100th Meridian almost to the Pacific slope it was a catastrophe," says John Clay. "The cowmen of the west and northwest were flat broke. Many of them never recovered. Most of the eastern men and the Britishers said 'enough' and went away. The big guns toppled over; the small ones had as much chance as a fly in molasses."

And over this lost land of the buffalo herds re-appeared that ghoulish army of a decade past, the old buffalo bone-pickers of the plains, now come to gather all that remained of the great cattle herds. The once flourishing ranges had been transformed into a boneyard.

After the winter of the Great Blizzard, only "the men with the bark on" came back to stay on the northwest ranges. A few of the big cattlemen survived, but in the years immediately following the disaster the grazing lands were rapidly fenced by hundreds of small ranchers homesteading claims. Many of the homesteaders were former cowboys who had lost their jobs with the bankrupt syndicates; others were eastern farmers who had moved farther west; some were outlaws, such as those driven out of Montana by Granville Stuart and the Stranglers.

Between the Big Horn Mountains and Powder River in Wyoming, the homesteaders soon became a political power, controlling Johnson County, with their headquarters in the county seat of Buffalo. South of Johnson County, the larger companies still ran thousands of cattle, the owners controlling Cheyenne and much of the political power of the state. Through the Wyoming Stock Growers' Association, which had been formed in Cheyenne in 1873, the cattlemen acted to keep the ranges open and to protect their property.

By 1890, friction between homesteaders and stockmen had reached a state of undeclared warfare. The stockmen believed they were entirely within their rights. They had come back after the Great Blizzard; by shrewd management and by risking borrowed capital they had rebuilt their herds. And now, they claimed, these herds were being rapidly decimated by their neighbors, the small ranchers, who seemed to delight in rustling and branding the big companies' stock in wholesale numbers.

The homesteaders, on the other hand, declared that the Cheyenne cattle kings were illegally using the best grasslands, and were invading their homesteads by force with patrols of gunmen.

In the preliminary skirmishes, the stockmen developed a new profession, that of the range detective, or range inspector. The range detectives led lives as dangerous as international spies, and spies they were in effect; most of them were former peace officers or hard-bitten gunmen imported from the declining trail towns of the southwest. Posing as ordinary cowhands, they secretly watched the homesteaders, reporting any evidences of stock thieving to their employers.

In spite of the best efforts of the range detectives, rustling increased all over Wyoming. Edgar Wilson (Bill) Nye, the nineteenth-century humorist who was editing the Laramie *Boomerang* in the early Eighties, summed up the situation in a single sentence: "Three years ago a guileless tenderfoot came to Wyoming, leading a single Texas steer and carrying a branding iron; now he is the opulent possessor of six hundred head of fine cattle—the ostensible progeny of that one steer."

Modeling a campaign after that of Granville Stuart and his Montana Stranglers, the Wyoming cattlemen arranged a few sporadic hangings. One of them involved a woman named Ella Watson who operated a small saloon in the Sweetwater River country.

Ella, the "Queen of the Sweetwater," was a buxom, good-natured blonde. Her business partner was Jim Averill, a pale-faced, scholarly man, who was supposedly a graduate of Cornell University. Jim liked to write letters to the Casper *Weekly Mail,* denouncing the cattle barons of Cheyenne in the libelous language that editors dared to print in those days. As their saloon business prospered, Ella changed her name to Kate Maxwell and purchased a small ranch nearby the saloon. From the evidence of both friends and enemies, it appears that she stocked it with mavericked steers traded to her by cowboys in exchange for her favors.

Cattle Kate's herd increased at such a rapid rate that range detectives were soon swarming around the Sweetwater saloon. Both Kate and Jim Averill were warned to leave the country, but they refused. One night in July, 1889, they were seized in their saloon and taken to Spring Creek Gulch, and hanged from a tree, their bodies left dangling over the gulch.

All northern Wyoming was immediately aroused. The Casper *Weekly Mail* reported the loss of its scholarly correspondent in headlines: JIM AVERILL, AN OLD RESIDENT OF SWEETWATER, HANGED TO A TREE. ELLA WATSON MEETS A SIMILAR FATE. CORONER'S JURY FINDS THAT PROMINENT LAND OWNERS ON SWEETWATER COMMIT THE ATROCIOUS DEED.

Six men were accused of the hangings, but no indictments were ever returned; one witness died and the others disappeared mysteriously before they could testify.

Violence spread across the ranges. Hanging followed hanging. In Buffalo, Frank Canton, a former sheriff who had taken a job with the Wyoming Stock Growers' Association as a range inspector, found himself a virtual prisoner within the town. The homesteaders suspected him of being responsible for several of the hangings. With the aid of four armed friends, Canton finally escaped and fled to Chicago.

To protect their property, the stockmen secured passage of new laws which set definite dates for all roundups, with state inspectors required to be present to oversee the branding. The homesteaders, however, were suspicious of the honesty of the state brand inspectors, and in the spring of 1892 decided to circumvent plans of the stockmen by ignoring the law and holding an early pool roundup in northern Wyoming.

This action was reported to the stockmen, and the Cheyenne Club began buzzing with wild rumors and secret meetings. Within a few days, some of the extremists among the cattlemen formed a society of Regulators, and drew up plans for a military invasion of Johnson County. As their leader, the Regulators selected a former army officer, Major Frank Wolcott, a hot-blooded Kentuckian who owned a large ranch on Deer Creek near the Platte. Wolcott was a stocky, domineering martinet, a master of the quick retort. At dinner one day he offered a visiting Texas cowboy some carrots. The Texan sniffed at Wolcott, and drawled: "We feed carrots to hogs down where I come from." "So do we," said Wolcott. "Have some."

Wolcott's chief lieutenant was Frank Canton, hastily summoned to Cheyenne from Chicago. Canton knew Johnson County better than any of the members of the Regulators, and he was offered a handsome price for his services.

Wolcott and Canton made quick trips to Colorado and the southwest to hire an army of gunmen, the best that could be found at a salary of five dollars a day and expenses, plus fifty dollars bonus for every homesteader they might kill during the invasion. In Denver, Wolcott rented a special train from the Union Pacific—an engine, one passenger car, one baggage car, and three freight cars. When the train reached Cheyenne, April 6, several stock cars filled with horses were added. During that day, guns, ammunition, dynamite, tents, blankets, and wagons were quietly moved into the freight cars.

Shortly after nightfall, fifty-two men armed with six-guns and rifles boarded the train. Several were well-known citizens of Wyoming; twenty-four were hired gunmen imported from the southwest. Dr. Charles Penrose signed on as official surgeon. The city editor of the Cheyenne *Sun* and a Chicago journalist went along as war correspondents.

BIG BLIZZARDS AND LITTLE WARS

At three o'clock in the morning, April 7, 1892, the little army arrived in Casper, end of the rail line. Telegraph wires to Buffalo were immediately cut, and scouts were sent ahead on fast horses.

Major Wolcott had prepared an exact military timetable, and supposedly a list of seventy homesteaders and rustlers, all of whom were scheduled to die before the "war" was to be declared ended. The timetable called for the army to arrive in Buffalo on April 9, where they would capture and publicly hang the sheriff, William H. (Red) Angus.

As they rode north from Casper under a gray blizzardy sky, what few travelers they met were immediately captured and forced to accompany the expedition, to prevent any news of the invasion being carried ahead of the advance. When they reached the Tisdale Ranch, on the border of Johnson County, Major Wolcott ordered a halt. Bob Tisdale, owner of the ranch, was accompanying the party, and the ranch stop was on Wolcott's timetable.

A short time later, Mike Shonsey, who had been scouting for the Regulators in Johnson County, arrived at the Tisdale Ranch with some interesting information. On the border of the Hole-in-the-Wall country, Shonsey had discovered two "rustlers" living at the K C Ranch. He said they were Nick Ray and Nate Champion.

Wolcott checked his list of seventy names. They were both there, Ray and Champion. The Major held a war council. A side stop at the K C Ranch was not on his timetable and might delay the scheduled arrival in Buffalo. But Nate Champion was an important leader of the homesteaders; he would have to be tracked down sooner or later. Wolcott decided to ride.

Ordering three of his best gunmen to act as guards for the drivers of the slow commissary wagons, he led the remainder of the expedition on a fast dash north to the Powder.

Meanwhile in the K C ranch house, Nick Ray and Nate Champion were playing hosts to two trappers, Bill Walker and Ben Jones, who had stopped over to spend the night. Champion was a friendly, powerfully built Texan, blue-eyed, sandy-haired, who had trailed Longhorns up the Goodnight-Loving route. Nick Ray was also a former cowboy. The partners had recently leased the K C Ranch, and like most of their neighbors had probably mavericked a few steers from the open ranges south of their spread.

After supper that evening, Champion got out a gallon jug of "snake juice," and trapper Bill Walker unpacked his old fiddle. The four men sat up late—singing, drinking, swapping stories, and looking through a new Montgomery Ward catalog.

Early the next morning, Champion started the breakfast fire and asked Ben Jones to fetch up a pail of fresh water from the river. Jones went out with the pail, but several minutes passed and he did not return. "Maybe you'd better go and hurry old Ben up," Champion said to Bill Walker. "I need that water for coffee right now."

Walker strolled down the trail toward the river. He saw a man crouched among the willows near the bank, then noticed that the horses in the corral had their heads up, ears pointed. Walker swung toward the barn.

"Hold it, pardner!"

Five rifle barrels bristled at him from the barn door. He stood in his tracks, astounded, until one of the gunmen brusquely ordered him to come inside, out of sight of the house.

Bill Walker had stepped right into the middle of Major Wolcott's army; they had already captured Ben Jones. And there was nothing the two trappers could do to warn Ray and Champion.

When Ray came outside a minute or two later, he was wounded by a volley from the Regulators' guns, but Champion managed to drag his partner back inside to temporary safety.

Champion was an excellent shot. In the middle of the afternoon he was still holding out against more than forty men. But Nick Ray was dead.

Shortly after three o'clock, Black Jack Flagg, a homesteader and editor from Buffalo, came riding by on horseback, trailing his stepson who was driving a light wagon. Flagg was puzzled over the firing, but not for long. When the Regulators began firing at him, he shouted to his stepson to jump on one of the team horses, then cut the harness, and the two galloped away, heading for Buffalo to sound the alarm.

Wolcott knew he would have to act fast now if he expected to keep the element of surprise in his timetable. He ordered an old wagon piled high with hay and pitchpine. After setting fire to the hay, four men rushed the wagon against the ranch house. Champion stayed inside as long as he could, then kicked off part of the burning roof and came crawling over the wall, with both his six-guns in action. When he tried to run for cover in a nearby draw, fire from twenty rifles burst upon him.

They found a short diary in one of Nate Champion's pockets, a record which he had kept during lulls in the fighting. He had included the names of some of his besiegers. But before the diary was replaced in the dead man's pocket, these names were cut out with a sharp penknife.

After pinning a placard, "CATTLE THIEVES BEWARE," to Nate Champion's coat, the Regulators rode away behind Major Wolcott who was shouting: "On to Buffalo!"

At that moment in Buffalo, however, another army was rapidly forming. Rumors of the invasion had reached Sheriff Red Angus before noon, and he had ordered posses formed. When Jack Flagg arrived to substantiate the rumors, the town was quickly transformed into a military base.

Bob Foote, the owner of Buffalo's largest general store, donned a theatrical black cape and mounted a stallion. Foote was a tall elderly man with white curly hair. He rode through the town, his long white beard flowing in the wind, exhorting the citizens to arise. "Come to my store," he shouted, "and get whatever you need for this battle. Fall in line!" He led a parade back to his store, opened it up, and began passing out guns and ammunition. Reverend M. A. Rader, a Buffalo minister, gathered a troop of forty armed churchmen. Arapaho Brown, a veteran Indian fighter, and E. U. Snider, a former sheriff, rode off to summon the outlying homesteaders.

Within a few hours, Sheriff Angus had an army of several hundred men, mounted and armed. The sheriff spent the night trying to get aid from the state militia and from regular army troops stationed at nearby Fort McKinney. But no assistance was offered him.

At dawn on the tenth day of April, Johnson County's army began moving south, as

230

strange an army as ever went to war; the sheriff's regular posse leading the advance, the volunteer homesteaders following.

About the same time, Major Wolcott's Regulators were preparing to march north into Buffalo. They had spent the night in the T A ranch house on Crazy Woman Creek, fourteen miles south of the town. Advance scouts, however, saw the homesteader army moving toward them, and the Regulators retreated rapidly back to the T A Ranch. In the short time left to them, Wolcott and his men prepared barricades and deployed for a siege.

The battle lasted for two days. Toward the end of the second day, Arapaho Brown began preparing a "go-devil" to finish off the Regulators. He chose a method similar to that used by Wolcott to smoke out Nate Champion. Dynamite surrounded by bales of hay was mounted on a wagon. But just as the homesteaders were moving their crude bomb slowly toward the T A ranch house, a bugle sounded from far up the trail to Buffalo.

No dime novel author ever contrived a more dramatic arrival of the United States cavalry. During the previous night, Wolcott had sneaked one of his best scouts out through the homesteaders' lines; the man had reached Fort McKinney, and now three troops of cavalry came riding to the rescue of the apparently doomed stockmen. The Johnson County invasion ended abruptly.

The United States cavalry had wanted no part of the war, but on orders from Washington, Colonel J. J. Van Horn, commanding the Fort McKinney troops, now had in his custody all the participants on one side of the conflict. Colonel Van Horn refused to turn his prisoners over to the Johnson County authorities; he knew well enough that if he did so, about fifty hangings would follow within a few hours.

The Regulators were taken to Fort D. A. Russell, and held for several weeks awaiting trial. All expenses for guards and food were charged against Johnson County until that county's treasury was exhausted. An application for a change of venue was then made, and the men were transferred to Cheyenne. Here their imprisonment became a farce, the prisoners employing their own guards, moving freely about town during the day and returning dutifully to their imposed jail at night. When the time for their trial came in January, 1893, no jurors acceptable to both sides could be found. Finally the case was dismissed, and so ended the Johnson County War.

Peace came slowly to the Wyoming ranges after 1893. It was obvious now to everyone that the day of the open range was almost over. Theodore Roosevelt had seen the end in 1888, when he wrote: "In its present form stock-raising on the plains is doomed, and can hardly outlast the century. The great free ranches, with their barbarous, picturesque, and curiously fascinating surroundings, mark a primitive stage of existence as surely as do the great tracts of primeval forests, and like the latter must pass away before the onward march of our people; and we who have felt the charm of the life, and have exulted in its abounding vigor and its bold, restless freedom, will not only regret its passing for our own sakes, but must also feel real sorrow that those who come after us are not to see, as we have seen, what is perhaps the pleasantest, healthiest, and most exciting phase of American existence."

But before the barbed wire fences sealed off the last of the northwestern trails, one more dramatic actor was to play out a significant role. His name was Tom Horn, and his passing definitely marked the end of the free range.

Tom Horn may have been a member of the Johnson County invasion force, escaping before the showdown at the T A Ranch. Bill Walker, one of the trappers captured at Nate Champion's ranch, later claimed that he saw Horn there, but the statement has never been proved. It is certain, however, that Horn did play a part in preparations for the invasion.

In 1890, after a remarkable and sometimes heroic career as an army scout in the Apache country of the southwest, Tom Horn had joined the Pinkerton Detective Agency in Denver. Two years later, when the Cheyenne Regulators were planning their raid against the northern homesteaders, he was selected to go to Arizona and employ a few desperadoes to join the invasion army. He also may have gone to Idaho on a similar mission.

In 1893, Horn's reputation for efficiency won him a job as a range detective with the Swan Land and Cattle Company, at that time managed by John Clay. On the company's books, Horn was listed as a cowhand employed to break horses. "I never fathomed his character," says Clay, who tells how Horn would come into the ranch office without making a sound, and then after passing the time of day would roll a cigarette, light it, and sit silent for long periods of time, braiding ropes of fine horse hair.

For the next few years, Tom Horn roamed the ranges of several of the big cattle companies as a cowpuncher, covering almost half of Wyoming. Whenever a cattleman suspected rustling, he quietly summoned this tall sunburned man with drooping, sharp-pointed mustaches. "Killing is my business," Horn remarked on several occasions. He operated alone, making his kills with a rifle, leaving two stones under the heads of his victims as a sort of signature. He worked for a flat fee of six hundred dollars. After each killing, it was his habit to drift into Cheyenne or Denver, and go on a big drunk. A silent man while sober, he became unusually loquacious during these periods. While Tom Horn was drunk he talked wildly, bragging of his skill as a killer.

When the Spanish-American War came along in 1898, Horn went to Cuba as master of a pack train. Many of his old army friends of the Apache campaigns were there, and for him the war was a long lively holiday.

In the spring of 1901, he returned to Wyoming and took a job with John Coble, a wealthy cattleman who operated a ranch north of Laramie near Iron Mountain. Coble suspected that some of the homesteaders who had claims adjoining his ranch were rustling from his stock, and he knew that Horn was the man who could put a sudden stop to the thieving.

Tom Horn took his time, scouting around and studying the neighbors. One day he rode casually up to the farmhouse of Victor Miller and got himself invited to supper. The Millers had a boarder, the Iron Mountain schoolteacher, Glendolene Kimmel, who had recently come west from Missouri. To Miss Kimmel, Tom Horn was a knight in shining armor, the western horseman she had dreamed of meeting when she accepted her schoolteaching contract.

But the tall killer was wary of schoolma'ams. He shied away from Glendolene Kimmel, and concentrated carefully on the Millers, feeling them out about Coble. Although the Millers had heard of Tom Horn's reputation, they spoke freely. They disliked Coble, and considered his big ranch an intrusion. But if they disliked the wealthy stockman, then their feelings for a neighboring homesteader, Kels P. Nickell, was pure hatred by comparison. Nickell and Miller had quarreled over land boundaries, the quarrel finally resulting in a fight in which Nickell had attacked Miller with a knife, wounding him seriously. After he recovered, Miller began carrying a loaded shotgun for protection. One day the shotgun slipped from its position on the wagon seat, went off accidentally, and killed one of Miller's sons. Miller told Tom Horn that Nickell was indirectly responsible for his boy's death, and that the score would not be even until one of Nickell's sons had been killed.

Horn listened quietly to Victor Miller's violent talk. He made several return visits, and became more friendly with Glendolene Kimmel. But he was also watching and listening to the Nickell family.

On July 18, Nickell's thirteen-year-old son, Willie, prepared to ride over to the family's sheep camp to spend the night. He told his mother goodbye at the door of the house. Twenty minutes later, two shots from a rifle killed thirteen-year-old Willie Nickell.

They found his body the next day. Two men were immediately suspected of the murder, Tom Horn and Victor Miller. Horn produced an alibi that he had been on a train between Laramie and Cheyenne on the day the boy was murdered. And the Miller family, supported by Glendolene Kimmel, swore that Victor Miller was at home the day of the killing. When she realized that Tom Horn might be endangered because of her testimony, Miss Kimmel immediately reversed her statement, and swore that Victor Miller had been absent from the house. No arrests were made.

Meanwhile the county and state had posted a thousand dollars reward for the capture of the murderer. A short, plump, mild-mannered marshal named Joe Lefors appeared at Iron Mountain, questioned everybody concerned, and soon made up his mind as to the identity of the killer. He immediately set to work to prove his case. He had known Tom Horn quite well, and did not believe the range detective would deliberately kill a small boy. When Kels Nickell was shot and wounded a short time later, Lefors guessed that Horn had killed Willie Nickell by mistake.

While Lefors was quietly gathering evidence, Tom Horn was in Denver on a big drunk. He finally woke up in a hospital with a broken jaw, the result of a bar-room brawl. Some time later he returned to Cheyenne and found awaiting him there a letter from Glendolene Kimmel warning him to beware of Joe Lefors.

Lefors soon found Horn, got him to drinking, then persuaded him to come up to his office to swap some talk in private. The marshal had two deputies concealed behind a thin partition, and while Tom Horn drank and talked out what seemed to be a confession of the Willie Nickell shooting, his words were being secretly recorded in shorthand.

The next morning Tom Horn was arrested. John Coble and other stockmen rallied to his aid; they employed a battery of lawyers to defend him and arranged a trial delay of four months to October, 1902.

On October 12, Cheyenne was crowded with cattlemen and homesteaders from all over the state, come to see Tom Horn's trial. Glendolene Kimmel arrived at the courthouse wearing a red tam-o'-shanter. John Coble was there, and Kels Nickell. Every important newspaper in the west had representatives present.

The trial lasted for two weeks, with sensational front-page news stories every day. Joe Lefors' shorthand record of Tom Horn's conversation clinched the argument for the prosecution. The jury found him guilty of murder in the first degree.

Horn shrugged off the judge's sentence "to be hanged by the neck until you are dead." He was not scheduled to die until January 9, and he was confident his friends would obtain a new trial for him. He sat in his cell braiding intricately designed horsehair ropes. He wrote the story of his life on five hundred large-sized letter pages.

A new trial was denied, but the execution date was postponed. His friends then arranged for a young cowboy to be arrested and confined for a few days in the jail. Through this boy, Tom Horn was to reveal a detailed plan of escape. He wrote the plan on pieces of toilet paper, rolling them into pellets and dropping them into the cowboy's cell.

But at the last moment, the youthful accomplice lost his nerve, and when he was freed he ran to a Cheyenne newspaperman and revealed the plot. The newspaper scooped not only its rivals but also the county sheriff.

Horn decided to escape anyhow. Working with another prisoner, he overpowered the guards, but before he could get outside the jail, a deputy spread an alarm. When Tom Horn dashed into the streets of Cheyenne, almost all the bells and whistles in town were jangling or shrieking. The veteran of a dozen Apache raids was ignominiously captured by a blue-coated policeman.

On November 15, 1903, Tom Horn's jailer informed him that he would hang five days later. No more postponements had been ordered. But Horn had received rumors that John Coble and an army of cowboys were in Cheyenne, and that Butch Cassidy and the Hole-in-the-Wall Gang had been hired to pull him out of the jail.

The Cheyenne authorities heard the same rumors. The governor ordered a troop of soldiers to patrol the courthouse square. A November blizzard had just swept across eastern Wyoming, leaving temperatures of forty below, but hundreds of spectators came to watch the patrolling soldiers and to see what would happen if the cowpunchers and Butch Cassidy's outlaws came swarming toward the jail.

On November 18, Tom Horn received a secret message that he would be freed on the nineteenth, one day before the scheduled execution. When he awoke on the morning of the nineteenth and looked out of his cell window, he saw three words marked into the snow: *Keep Your Nerve*. But all day long as he sat waiting he could hear the sheriff and his deputies at work on the gallows.

Glendolene Kimmel, with a pack of statements swearing to the innocence of her hero, went to see the governor that day, but the governor refused to read them. And throughout that night, Cheyenne's saloons stayed open, the gamblers giving odds that Tom Horn would be freed before morning.

But the man who had survived attacks from deadly Apaches, from sure-shot train robbers, and from a hundred skulking enemies on the cattle ranges—was officially hanged on schedule the morning of November 20, 1903.

Before nightfall, rumors were all over Laramie County that Tom Horn had not really been hung. And in parts of Wyoming today, old-timers will solemnly swear a last-minute switch was made, and that in some lonely place up a remote canyon somewhere one may find today a white-haired old man hiding out in a cabin, braiding intricate horsehair riatas to pass the time away.

In the fifteen years following the Great Blizzard, changes had come so rapidly on the western rangelands that the old trail drivers could scarcely realize what had happened. Deep wells and windmills, pasture planting and hay mowing, de-horning and fence-stretching, and sheep—whole herds of sheep running on the same ranges with cattle! Ranch life had certainly changed.

One old cowhand summed it up for the Sidney (Texas) *Independent:* "Cowboys don't have as soft a time as they did eight or ten years ago," he said. "I remember when we set around the fire the winter through and didn't do a lick of work for five or six months of the year, except to chop a little wood to build a fire to keep warm by. Now we go to the general roundup, then the calf roundup, then comes haying—something that the old-time cowboy never dreamed of—then the beef roundup and fall calf roundup, and gathering bulls and weak cows, and after all this a winter of feeding hay. I tell you times have changed. You didn't hear the sound of a mowing machine in this country ten years ago. We didn't have any hay, and the man who thinks he is going to strike a soft job now in a cow camp is woefully left."

The trail driving days were gone forever, and all that was left were the names strewn across the land—Sweetgrass and Ogallala, Tensleep and Powder River, Boot Hill and Turkey Track, Abilene and Bitterroot. Rawhide Creek and Sweetwater, Texas Street and Horse Thief Creek, Medicine Bow and Chisholm Trail, Red River and Hat Creek, the Chugwater and the Pecos, Whoopup and Box Elder, Kaycee and Badwater, the Palo Duro and Dodge City.

These and a hundred other evocative and musical names will forever remain, symbols of the long gone, golden days of the old trail driving cattlemen.

DRY RANGE

At summer's end of the year 1886, the weather was unusual. Except for the chill nights, dry warm temperatures kept the cowboys in their shirtsleeves, and autumn came to Indian Summer with no break of frost. The range was dry, and the smokes of many grass fires lay over the land from the Yellowstone to the Texas Panhandle.

CONRAD KOHRS

In Montana, rancher Conrad Kohrs fought range fires through the autumn, but so much grass was burned he knew his cattle could not survive the winter. He asked the Canadian government for permission to graze across the line into Canada, and prepared to move his herds north.

Conrad Kohrs was one of Montana's first and greatest ranchers, establishing a pioneer herd from cattle collected along the old California and Oregon trails. He operated ranches on the Sun River range and on the Tongue River below Miles City.

CATTLE IN CANADA (above)

Drouths in Wyoming's Powder River valley brought herds north into Montana, but these soon joined Conrad Kohr's outfit across the Canadian border.

PRELUDE TO THE GREAT BLIZZARD
  (below)

On the 16th of November 1886, the thermometer dropped below zero over the Rockies. A northwest wind broke the long strange silence of the warm autumn, drifting six inches of fine snow across the dry ranges of the northwest.

237

"A TORNADO OF WHITE FROZEN DUST"

On January 28, 1887, the Great Blizzard struck the northwest. For seventy-two hours, it seemed as if all the world's ice had come on a wind that howled and screamed with the fury of demons. It was a tornado of white frozen dust. When the storm ended, millions of open range cattle were scattered for miles, dead or dying in the deep drifts.

SNOW-BOUND TRAIN ON THE NORTHERN PACIFIC (*on facing page, top*)

All life and movement was suspended. Trains were blocked. Towns were isolated for weeks. Whole families were frozen to death in their cabins.

LAST OF THE FIVE THOUSAND (*on facing page*)

Charles M. Russell, the northwest's cowboy artist, was managing a herd of 5,000 cattle in the Judith Basin during that winter. The ranch owner, who lived in Helena, wrote Russell for a report on the herd's condition. Unable to find words to describe the situation, Russell drew the sketch (*at right*) on a postcard

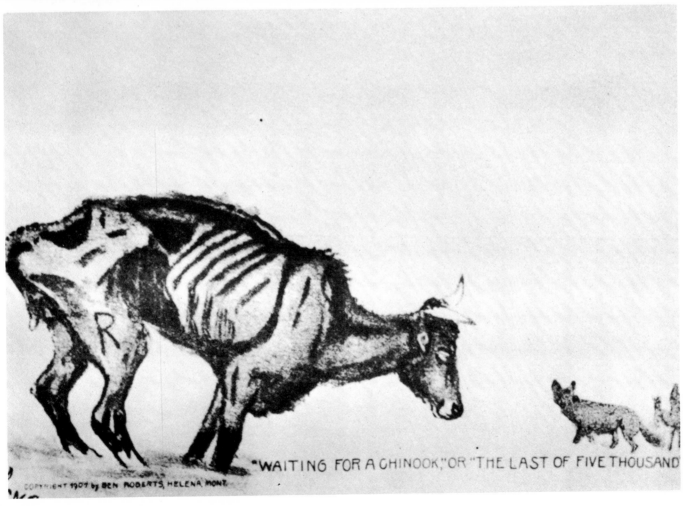

"WAITING FOR A CHINOOK," OR "THE LAST OF FIVE THOUSAND"

COPYRIGHT 1907 by BEN ROBERTS, HELENA, MONT.

AFTERMATH

Finally in March, the sun burned through the cold gray haze. As the snow retreated, the cattlemen could count their losses, and in that dismal spring of 1887 many a grotesque and terrible discovery was made on the ranges of the northwest.

ABANDONED RANCH HOUSE (*on facing page, top*)

Many a ranch was deserted forever. The gay young men of Cheyenne lost their zest for cattle raising and departed the country. Thousands of cowboys lost their jobs, and to earn their bread joined the despised nesters in staking claims for homesteads. Banks failed, stockyards closed. The spring roundups were gloomy affairs.

RETURN OF THE BONE PICKERS (*on facing page*)

Over the lost land of the buffalo herds re-appeared that ghoulish army of a decade past, the old buffalo bone pickers of the plains, now come to gather all that remained of the great cattle herds. The once flourishing range had been transformed into a boneyard for the fertilizer factories.

241

BEN MORRISON, RANGE DETECTIVE

The big cattle companies which survived the Great Blizzard were plagued by a sharp increase in rustling. To protect their stock, the cattlemen employed range detectives. Ben Morrison was one of the first, and he led a life as dangerous as that of an international spy.

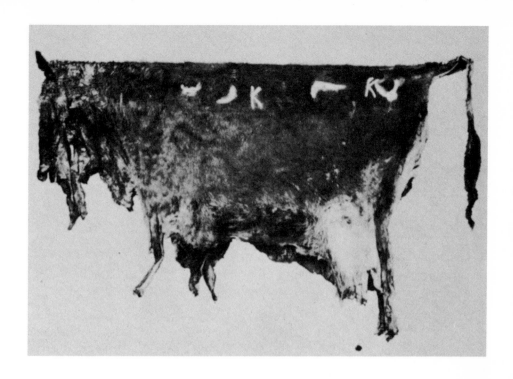

EXHIBIT A (*above*)

In the preliminary skirmishes between the stockmen and the homesteaders, charges of rustling were taken to the courts for settlement. To prove brand alterations, the detectives often removed hides from stolen cattle. The inner side of a hide would reveal the original owner's brand, which a clever blotcher with a running iron might have changed and concealed on the outside.

N. K. BOSWELL (*below*)

N. K. Boswell, chief of range detectives, attempted to break up an outlaw gang operating from the Hole-in-the-Wall country. The outlaws used the struggle between homesteaders and range cattlemen as a cover for their wholesale rustling.

THE HANGINGS BEGIN—
CATTLE KATE AND JIM AVERILL

Conditions became so bad in the Sweetwater River area that the cattlemen decided to stage a few hangings outside the law. Ella Watson *alias* Cattle Kate Maxwell and her partner, Jim Averill, were suspected of rustling. One night in July 1889, they were seized and hanged.

FRANK CANTON

Violence spread across the ranges. Frank Canton, a stock detective, found himself a virtual prisoner in Buffalo, county seat of Johnson County and political stronghold of the homesteaders. With the aid of four armed friends, Canton finally escaped.

MAJOR FRANK WOLCOTT

In the spring of 1892, Major Frank Wolcott was selected as leader of a group of angry Cheyenne cattlemen who called themselves the Regulators. Major Wolcott and Frank Canton began planning a military invasion of Johnson County.

HOLE-IN-THE-WALL RANCH

The first objective of the army was the Hole-in-the-Wall country, where homesteaders had established small ranches adjoining the big cattle companies' ranges. The invaders hoped to capture and hang Nate Champion and Nick Ray, two former cowboys who had leased the K C Ranch.

BILL WALKER

Bill Walker, friend of Ray and Champion, was one of the first men captured by the army from Cheyenne. He was trapped outside the K C ranch house, and was unable to warn the others.

LAST EDITION   DENVER, COLORAD

A BATTLE!

Forty-Six Men Killed in Wyoming Yesterday.

THE REPORT IS BELIEVED.

The News Causes Intense Excitement at Casper.

THE DETERMINED RUSTLERS.

The Factions Will Fight Until Not a Live Man Remains.

SOME CONFLICTING RUMORS.

Friends of Each Side Are Rushing to the Scene of Action—Very Sensational News—More Conflicts Certain.

CASPER, Wyo., April 12.—(Special)—Late last night a man from Riverside arrived here and reported that the 150 deputies of Sheriff Angus attempted to arrest the invading army and killed 28 of them, and 18 of their own men were killed.

Great excitement prevails here.

No one knows who the armed force is after nor what moment they may swoop down upon this community.

The town is a walking arsenal. If the ringleader's object is to kill off all his private enemies on this trip, about one-half the population must be on the list. This section to a man will turn out if any miscellaneous killing takes place around here.

Several newspaper representatives are here, but fear to go to the scene, as everything is looked upon with suspicion, and the army, if they caught the reporters, would keep them close prisoners.

NATE CHAMPION'S MEN.

An Account of the Conflict from Gillette, Wyo.

GILLETTE, Wyo., April 12.—(Special)—Nate Champion and 50 men are surrounded by 100 men, under Fred Hesse and Charles Ford, at the T. A. ranch. Two hundred shots have been discharged, but the damage done on either side cannot be ascertained.

The fighting is done with Winchesters and in a fashion long range. Sheriff Angus and posse, who left yesterday for Montana river, are cut off from town.

A number of men are known to have been wounded and some killed. About 100 rustlers have passed through town en route to the scene of the battle to help Champion and his men.

A TEST CASE.

Constitutionality of the Bounty Law Before the Supreme Court.

The test case started in the district court of El Paso county to test the constitutionality of the bounty law was filed in the supreme court several days ago and the judges have been asked to advance it on the docket and have the same under consideration now.

This case will be of interest in every county in the state as all are called upon to pay bounty on loco weed and wolf, coyote, bear or mountain lion scalps. If the court decides the law unconstitutional county treasurers will have to turn the funds into the state treasury instead of paying the entire amount in bounties, as is the case in some counties. It costs the state about $40,000 a year for bounties.

AT CRIPPLE CREEK.

Fremont Preparing for the Big Pueblo Excursion.

FREMONT, Colo., April 12.—(Special)—Extensive preparations are being made here for the reception of the Pueblo excursion, which will be in this evening. A bag of samples from the various producing mines will be given the visitors as souvenirs of the camp.

The flagpole at the intersection of Bennet and Second streets was raised this morning, and the mineral pyramids are being erected. The pole is 83 feet and six inches high, and is as straight as an arrow and without a splice. It was cut near the city and is considered one of the finest pieces of timber ever seen.

BAD JOHN O'DONNELL.

An Ex-Denver Policeman and His Bigamous Career.

BURDENS OF WIFE NO. 2.

How O'Donnell Came Back from California and Abused Her—She Asks Protection—A Very Sad Story.

When a man, who has two wives living, abuses wife No. 2 because she repudiates him after the discovery of the existence of No. 1, it exhibits a breadth of gall which is marvelous in its magnitude. But there is little doubt that John O'Donnell, formerly a Denver policeman, recently of California, is doing that very thing every day at 650 Clear Creek avenue, North Denver.

Seven years ago O'Donnell married the Denver Mrs. O'Donnell. The lady had been married before and had a daughter now 15 years of age. Her husband was not always the kindest and his wife had many burdens to bear, but she was patient and did not murmur.

For a long time O'Donnell was on the police force, but he got to drinking too hard and many complaints were lodged against him

FEARFUL!

Terrible Floods in Northern Mississippi.

NUMBERLESS FATALITIES.

The Water Came Upon Them Without Warning.

TWENTY-SIX DEAD BODIES.

One Man Gathers an Awful Boatload.

LOSS A MILLION DOLLARS.

The Appalling Character of the Disaster Just Becoming Known—Hundreds of Lives Lost—Raging Torrents and Inland Seas.

ST. LOUIS, April 12.—A special from Nashville, Tenn., to the Post-Dispatch says: The appalling character of the floods in northern Mississippi is just beginning to be realized Hundreds of lives have been lost.

Last night one man rowed several miles in the dark in a skiff with 26 bodies he had picked up.

The flood came so suddenly that none were prepared.

Sixteen small streams in northern Mississippi became raging torrents within a few hours and swelled the already full banks of the Coosa and Tom Bigbee rivers into inland seas.

All sorts of crafts are being improvised to go to the rescue of the survivors, who are perched on the highest ground without food or shelter.

The loss of property is incalculable at present. There is no exaggeration in the statement, however, that it will be over $1,000,000.

THE REPORT CONFIRMED.

The Loss of Life Will Reach Two Hundred.

ST. LOUIS, April 12.—A special from New Orleans to the Post-Dispatch says: The reported loss of life and property by the floods in Tom Bigbee river has been confirmed.

The citizens of Loundes county, Miss., have petitioned Congressman Allen, their representative, to ask the government for aid, as their own means are inadequate to the needs of the homeless people.

The losses of life are variously estimated at from 50 to 200.

A BATTLE!

Nick Ray and Nate Champion were besieged in the ranch house until both men were killed. But during the battle, a homesteader named Black Jack Flagg happened to ride past. He dashed away towards Buffalo to spread the alarm. As all telegraph wires had been cut by the invading cattlemen, the Cheyenne and Denver newspapers could print only the wildest of rumors.

247

BUFFALO, WYOMING

In Buffalo, meanwhile, another army was forming. Shortly after Black Jack Flagg arrived with news of the fight on the K C Ranch, the little town was transformed into a military base.

SHERIFF ANGUS AND
ARAPAHO BROWN

At dawn on April 10th, Sheriff Red Angus led an army of several hundred homesteaders south to meet Major Wolcott's Regulators. The Cheyenne stockmen were trapped behind barricades at the T A Ranch.

Arapaho Brown, veteran Indian fighter, built a dynamite "go-devil" on a hay wagon, and warned the invaders to surrender or die.

THE CAPTIVE CATTLEMEN

Just as all seemed lost for the besieged cattlemen, the United States Cavalry arrived to rescue them. They were taken to Fort McKinney as prisoners.

After their transfer to Cheyenne, the cattlemen maintained a pretense of being prisoners. But when the time came for the trial in January 1893, no jurors acceptable to both sides could be found. Finally the case was dismissed, and so ended the Johnson County War.

TOM HORN

As the last of the free ranges were being closed off, Tom Horn, famed army scout and range detective, was playing out a fitting dramatic role. In July 1901, the legendary Horn became involved in the killing of young Willie Nickell, son of a homesteader.

JOE LEFORS GETS HIS MAN

When a large reward was posted for the capture of Willie Nickell's murderer, Marshall Joe Lefors took up the chase. He soon had Tom Horn behind bars. After months of legal wrangling and wild rumors of new range wars, the veteran scout was finally hanged. His death marked the end of the open range.

TOM HORN IN JAIL

RANCH CHORE: DE-HORNING (*on facing page, top*)

In the fifteen years following the Great Blizzard, changes had come so rapidly on the western rangelands that the old trail drivers could scarcely realize what had happened.

Now there was work to be done the year around. Cattle had to be de-horned to keep down losses from goring, deep wells had to be dug for water, fences had to be stretched.

"I TELL YOU, TIMES HAVE CHANGED" (*on facing page*)

One old cowhand summed it up as follows:
"I tell you, times have changed. You didn't hear the sound of a mowing machine in this country ten years ago. We didn't have any hay, and the man who thinks he is going to strike a soft job now in a cow camp is woefully left."

"WAKE UP AND PAY FOR YOUR BED!" (*above*)

Civilization was intruding with all its superfluous comforts, and the dude ranch was not far away when working cowboys began packing mattresses on the roundups. The old chuckwagon drivers cursed the extra loads of gear—but the past was gone, gone, and no man could bring it back again.

NAMES ACROSS THE LAND

All that was left were the names strewn across the land—Sweetgrass and Ogallala, Tensleep and Powder River, Boot Hill and Turkey Track, Abilene and Bitterroot, Rawhide Creek and Sweetwater, Texas Street and Horse Thief Creek, Medicine Bow and Chisholm Trail, and Red River and Hat Creek, the Chugwater and the Pecos, Whoopup and Box Elder, Kaycee and Badwater, the Palo Duro and Dodge City.

But these and a hundred other evocative and musical names will forever remain, symbols of the long gone, golden days of the old trail driving cattlemen.

$\mathcal{Bibliography}$

———◄◄❂─❧❀❧─❂►►———

I. BOOKS

Abbott, Edward C. and Helena H. Smith
We Pointed Them North: Recollections of a Cowpuncher. New York, Farrar & Rinehart, 1939.

Adair, Cornelia
My Diary. Bath, England, 1918.

Adams, Andy
Cattle Brands. Boston, Houghton, 1906.

Adams, Andy
Log of a Cowboy. Boston, Houghton, 1927.

Adams, Ramon F.
Western Words: a Dictionary of the Range, Cow Camp and Trail. Norman, University of Oklahoma Press, 1945.

Aldridge, Reginald
Life on a Ranch: Ranch Notes in Kansas, Colorado, the Indian Territory and Northern Texas. New York, Appleton, 1884.

Allen, Jules V.
Cowboy Lore. San Antonio, Naylor, 1933.

Allen, Lewis F.
American Cattle; Their History, Breeding and Management. New York, Taintor Bros., 1881.

Angell, George T.
Cattle Transportation in the United States. Boston, 1872.

Applegate, Jesse
A Day with the Cow Column in 1843. Chicago, Caxton, 1934.

Armour, J. Ogden
The Packers, the Private Car Lines & the People. Philadelphia, Altemus, 1906.

Armour, Philip D.
The Present Condition of the Live Cattle and Beef Markets in the United States. Chicago, Legal News Co., 1889.

Arnold, Oren
Hot Irons: Heraldry of the Range. New York, Macmillan, 1940.

Artrip, Louise and Fullen
Memoirs of Daniel Fore (Jim) Chisholm and the Chisholm Trail. Booneville, Ark., Artrip Publications, 1949.

Atchison, Topeka and Santa Fe Railroads
Documents Relating To . . . Boston, 1890-93. 3 vols.

Babbitt, A. T. and Others
Cattle Brands Owned by Members of the Wyoming Stock Growers' Association. Chicago, 1882.

Baber, D. F.
The Longest Rope, the Truth About the Johnson County Cattle War. Caldwell, Idaho, Caxton, 1940.

Baillie-Grohman, William A.
Camps in the Rockies. New York, Scribners, 1882.

Bakarich, Sarah Grace
Gun Smoke. Tombstone, Arizona, 1947.

Ballinger, R. H.
Does It Pay? Larned, Kansas, Chronoscope Job Print, 1883.

Barnes, William C.
Apaches and Longhorns. Los Angeles, Ward Ritchie, 1941.

Barnes, William C.
Story of the Range. Washington, D. C., U. S. Dept. of Agriculture, 1926.

Barnes, William C.
Tales from the X-Bar Horse Camp. Chicago, Breeders' Gazette, 1920.

Barnes, William C.
Western Grazing Grounds and Forest Ranges: a History of the Livestock Industry as Conducted on the Open Ranges of the Arid West. Chicago, Breeders' Gazette, 1913.

Beadle, John H.
The Undeveloped West, or Five Years in the Territories. Philadelphia, National Publishing Co., 1873.

Bechdolt, Frederick R.
Tales of the Old Timers. New York, Century, 1924.

Bell, J. G.
Log of the Texas-California Trail, 1854. Edited by J. Evatts Haley. Austin, Texas, 1932.

255

BIBLIOGRAPHY

Bennett, Russell H.
The Compleat Rancher. New York, Rinehart, 1946.

Benton, Frank
Cowboy Life on the Sidetrack. Denver, Western Stories Syndicate, 1903.

Beverly, Bob
Hobo of the Rangeland. Lovington, New Mexico, n.d.

Biggers, Don H.
From Cattle Range to Cotton Patch. Bandera, Texas, 1944.

Black, A. P.
The End of the Longhorn Trail. Selfridge, North Dakota, Selfridge Journal, n.d.

Bowles, Samuel
Our New West. Hartford, Hartford Publishing Company, 1869.

Branch, Edward Douglas
The Cowboy and His Interpreters. New York, Appleton, 1926.

Bratt, John
Trails of Yesterday. Lincoln, Nebraska, University Publishing Co., 1921.

Breakenridge, William M.
Helldorado. Boston, Houghton, 1928.

Briggs, Harold E.
Frontiers of the Northwest. New York, Appleton-Century, 1940.

Brininstool, Earl
Trail Dust of a Maverick. New York, Dodd Mead, 1914.

Brisbin, James S.
The Beef Bonanza. Philadelphia, Lippincott, 1881.

Bronson, Edgar Beecher
Cowboy Life on the Western Plains. New York, Grosset and Dunlap, 1910.

Bronson, Edgar Beecher
The Red-Blooded. Chicago, McClurg, 1910.

Bronson, Edgar Beecher
Reminiscences of a Ranchman. Chicago, McClurg, 1910.

Brown, John Henry
History of Texas. St. Louis, L. E. Daniell, 1892-93.

Brush, Wilmot Proviso
Brandbook Containing the Brands of the Cherokee Strip. Kansas City, Moore, 1882.

Burdick, Usher L.
Marquis de Mores at War in the Bad Lands. Fargo, North Dakota, 1929.

Burney, John H.
Memoirs of a Cow Pony as Told by Himself. Boston, Eastern Publishing Co., 1906.

Burns, Walter Noble
The Saga of Billy the Kid. Garden City, N. Y., Doubleday, 1926.

Burt, Maxwell Struthers
Powder River. New York, Farrar & Rinehart, 1938.

Burton, Harley True
History of the J A Ranch. Austin, Von Boeckmann-Jones Co., 1928.

Canton, Frank M.
Frontier Trails: the Autobiography of Frank M. Canton. Edited by Edward Everett Dale. Boston, Houghton, 1930.

Carr, Robert V.
Cowboy Lyrics. Boston, Small, Maynard & Co., 1912.

A Century of Texas Cattle Brands. Fort Worth, 1936.

Chapman, Arthur
Out Where the West Begins. Boston, Houghton, 1917.

Clark, Charles Badger
Sun and Saddle Leather. Boston, Badger, 1922.

Clark, O. S.
Clay Allison of the Washita. Attica, Indiana, G. M. Williams, 1922.

Clay, John
My Life on the Range. Chicago, privately printed, 1924.

Clemen, Rudolph A.
The American Livestock and Meat Industry. New York, Ronald Press, 1923.

Coburn, Wallace David
Rhymes from a Round-up Camp. New York, Putnam, 1903.

Colbert, Walter
The Cattle Industry: What It Is Now and What It Was 65 to 70 Years Ago. Ardmore, Oklahoma, 1941.

Collings, Ellsworth
The 101 Ranch. Norman, University of Oklahoma Press, 1937.

Collins, Hubert E.
Warpath and Cattle Trail. New York, Morrow, 1928.

Colorado Brand Book. Denver, 1887.

Conard, Howard Louis
Uncle Dick Wootton. Chicago, Dibble, 1890.

Conn, William
Cowboys and Colonels. London, Griffith, Farran, Okedon and Welsh, n.d.

Connelly, William E.
Wild Bill and His Era. New York, Press of the Pioneers, 1933.

Cook, James H.
Fifty Years on the Old Frontier. New Haven, Yale University Press, 1923.

Cook, James H.
Longhorn Cowboy. New York, Putnam, 1942.

Cook, John R.
The Border and the Buffalo. Topeka, Kansas, Crane & Co., 1907.

Coolidge, Dane
Arizona Cowboys. New York, Dutton, 1938.

Coolidge, Dane
Old California Cowboys. New York, Dutton, 1939.

Coolidge, Dane
Texas Cowboys. New York, Dutton, 1937.

Coutant, C. G.
History of Wyoming. Laramie, Chaplin, Spafford and Mathison, 1899.

Cox, James
Historical and Biographical Record of the Cattle Industry and the Cattlemen of Texas and Adjacent Territory. St. Louis, Woodward & Tiernan, 1895.

Craig, John R.
Ranching with Lords and Commons, or Twenty Years on the Range. Toronto, privately printed, 1903.

Crawford, Lewis F.
Badlands and Broncho Trails. Bismarck, North Dakota, 1922.

Crawford, Lewis F.
Rekindling Camp Fires. Bismarck, North Dakota, 1926.

Crawford, Samuel Johnson
Kansas in the Sixties. Chicago, McClurg, 1911.

Crissey, F.
Alexander Legge. Chicago, privately printed, 1936.

Cross, F. J.
The Free Lands of Dakota. Yankton, 1876.

Cross, Joe
Cattle Clatter: History of Cattle from the Creation to the Texas Centennial in 1936. Kansas City, Walker Publishing Co., 1938.

Culley, John H.
Cattle, Horses and Men of the Western Range. Los Angeles, Ward Ritchie, 1940.

Cunningham, Eugene
Triggernometry: a Gallery of Gunfighters. New York, Press of the Pioneers, 1934.

Dale, Edward Everett
Cow Country. Norman, University of Oklahoma Press, 1942.

Dale, Edward Everett
The Range Cattle Industry. Norman, University of Oklahoma Press, 1930.

David, Robert B.
Finn Burnett. Glendale, Arthur H. Clark, 1937.

Davis, John Patterson
The Union Pacific Railway. Chicago, S. C. Griggs and Co., 1894.

Dayton, Edson C.
Dakota Days, May 1886-August 1898. Hartford, 1937.

De Lacy Lacy, Charles
The History of the Spur. n.p., n.d.

Dimsdale, Thomas J.
The Vigilantes of Montana. Helena, 1915.

Dobie, J. Frank
The Longhorns. Boston, Little, Brown, 1941.

Dobie, J. Frank
Mustangs and Cowhorses. Austin, Texas, Texas Folklore Society, 1940.

Dobie, J. Frank
On the Open Range. Dallas, Southwest Press, 1931.

Dobie, J. Frank
Tales of the Mustang. Dallas, Book Club of Texas, 1936.

Dobie, J. Frank
A Vaquero of the Brush Country. Dallas, Southwest Press, 1929.

Dodge, Richard Irving
The Hunting Grounds of the Great West. London, Chatto & Windus, 1877.

Donoho, M. H.
Circle Dot. Topeka, Crane & Co., 1907.

Doubleday, Russell
Cattle-ranch to College. New York, Doubleday and McClure, 1899.

Douglas, C. L.
Cattle Kings of Texas. Dallas, Regional Press, 1938.

Duval, John C.
Early Times in Texas. Austin, Gannel, 1892.

Dyer, Mrs. D. B.
Fort Reno. New York, G. W. Dillingham, 1896.

Edwards, J. B.
Early Days in Abilene. Abilene, 1938.

Ellard, Harry
Ranch Tales of the Rockies. Canyon City, Colorado, 1899.

Elliot, William J.
The Spurs. Spur, Texas, The Texas Spur, 1939.

Ellis, Edward S.
Cowmen and Rustlers: a Story of the Wyoming Cattle Ranges in 1892. Philadelphia, Coates, 1898.

Ellis, Edward S.
The Great Cattle Trail. Philadelphia, Coates, 1894.

Farley, Frank Webster
Raising Beef Cattle on Farm and Range. Kansas City, Missouri, Walker Publications, Inc., 1931.

Foy, Eddie and Harlow, Alvin F.
Clowning Through Life. New York, Dutton, 1928.

French, William
Some Recollections of a Western Ranchman: New Mexico 1883-1889. New York, Stokes, 1928.

Frewen, Moreton
Melton Mowbray and Other Memories. London, Jenkins, 1924.

Gann, Walter
Tread of the Longhorns. San Antonio, Naylor, 1949.

Garrett, Pat F.
The Authentic Life of Billy, the Kid . . . Santa Fe, New Mexico, New Mexican Printing and Publishing Co., 1882.

Gibson, J. Watt
Recollections of a Pioneer. St. Joseph, Missouri, privately printed, 1912.

Gillett, J. B.
Six years with the Texas Rangers, 1876-1881. Austin, Van Broeckman-Jones Co., 1921.

Goodnight, Charles, and Others
Pioneer Days in the Southwest, 1850-1879. Guthrie, Oklahoma, 1909.

Grand, W. Joseph
Illustrated History of the Union Stockyards. Chicago, 1896.

Greeley, Horace
An Overland Journey from New York to San Francisco in 1859. New York, Saxton, Barker & Co., 1860.

Greenburg, Dan W.
Sixty Years: a Brief Review of the Cattle Industry in Wyoming. Cheyenne, Wyoming Stock Growers' Association, 1932.

Grinnell, J. B.
The Cattle Industries of the United States. New York, Jos. H. Reall, 1882.

Guernsey, Charles A.
Wyoming Cowboy Days. New York, Putnam, 1936.

Hagedorn, Herman
Roosevelt in the Bad Lands. Boston, Houghton, 1921.

Hale, Will
24 Years a Cowboy and Ranchman in Southern Texas and Old Mexico. n.p., O. T. Hedrick and W. H. Stone, 1905.

Haley, J. Evetts
Charles Goodnight, Cowman and Plainsman. Boston, Houghton, 1936.

Haley, J. Evetts
George W. Littlefield, Texan. Norman, University of Oklahoma Press, 1943.

Haley, J. Evetts
The Heraldry of the Range. Canyon, Texas, Panhandle-Plains Historical Society, 1949.

Haley, J. Evetts
Jeff Milton: a Good Man with a Gun. Norman, University of Oklahoma Press, 1948.

Haley, J. Evetts
The XIT Ranch. Chicago, Lakeside Press, 1929.

Halsell, H. H.
Cowboys and Cattleland. Nashville, Tennessee, Parthenon Press, 1937.

Hamner, Laura Vernon
The No-gun Man of Texas, 1835-1929. Amarillo, Texas, 1935.

Hamner, Laura Vernon
Short Grass and Longhorns. Norman, University of Oklahoma Press, 1943.

Hardin, John Wesley
Life of . . . Written by Himself. Seguin, Texas, Smith & Moore, 1896.

Harper, Minnie Timms and Harper, George Dewey
Old Ranches. Dallas, Texas, Dealey and Lowe, 1936.

Harris, Frank
My Reminiscences as a Cowboy. New York, Boni, 1930.

Hastings, Frank S.
A Ranchman's Recollections. Chicago, Breeders' Gazette, 1921.

Hebard, Grace R. and Brininstool, Earl
The Bozeman Trail. Cleveland, A. H. Clark, 1924.

Hendricks, George David
The Bad Men of the West. San Antonio, Naylor, 1941.

Henry, Stuart
Conquering Our Great American Plains. New York, Dutton, 1930.

Hill, J. L.
The End of the Cattle Trail. Long Beach, California, G. W. Moyle, 1923.

Hill, Luther B.
History of the State of Oklahoma. Chicago, Lewis Publishing Co., 1908.

Hinkle, J. F.
   Early Days of a Cowboy on the Pecos. Roswell, New Mexico, 1937.
Holden, William Curry
   Alkali Trails. Dallas, Southwest Press, 1930.
Holden, William Curry
   The Spur Ranch. Boston, Christopher, 1934.
Hough, Emerson
   North of 36. New York, Appleton, 1929.
Hough, Emerson
   Story of the Cowboy. New York, Appleton, 1924.
Hough, Emerson
   The Story of the Outlaw. New York, Outing Publishing Company, 1907.
Howard, Joseph Kinsey
   Montana: High Wide and Handsome. New Haven, Yale University Press, 1944.
Huidekoper, Wallis
   The Land of the Dakotas, Helena, Montana, n.d.
Hunter, J. Marvin, ed.
   The Trail Drivers of Texas. 2nd ed., revised. Nashville, Cokesbury Press, 1925.
Inman, Henry
   The Old Santa Fe Trail. Topeka, Crane & Company, 1899.
Jackson, A. P., and Cole, E. C.
   Oklahoma. Kansas City, Millett & Hudson, 1885.
Jackson, W. H., and Long, S. A.
   The Texas Stock Directory, or Book of Marks and Brands. San Antonio, Herald Office, 1865.
James, W. S.
   Cowboy Life in Texas, or 27 Years a Mavrick. Chicago, Donahue, 1898.
James, Will
   Cow Country. New York, Scribners, 1931.
James, Will
   Cowboys North and South. New York, Scribners, 1924.
James, Will
   Lone Cowboy. New York, Scribners, 1930.
James, Will
   Sand. New York, A. L. Burt, 1929.
James, Will
   Smoky, the Cowhorse. New York, Scribners, 1926.
Jaques, Mary J.
   Texan Ranch Life. London, Horace Cox, 1894.
Johnson, Francis W.
   A History of Texas and Texans. Chicago, American Historical Society, 1918.
Johnson, Phil
   Life on the Plains. Chicago, 1888.

Kansas and Pacific Railway Company
   Guide map of the best and shortest cattle trail to the Kansas Pacific Railway. Kansas City, Missouri, Ramsey, Millett and Hudson, 1874.
Kansas City Stockyards Company
   Seventy-five Years of Kansas City Livestock Market History, 1871-1946. Kansas City, Missouri, 1946.
King, Edward
   The Southern States of North America. London, Blackie & Son, 1875.
King, Frank M.
   Pioneer Western Empire Builders. Pasadena, Calif., Trail's End Publishing Co., 1946.
Knibbs, Henry Herbert
   Songs of the Trail. Boston, Houghton, 1920.
LaFrentz, F. W.
   Cowboy Stuff. New York, Putnam, 1927.
Lake, Stuart
   Wyatt Earp, Frontier Marshal. Boston, Houghton, 1931.
Lampman, C. P.
   Great Western Trail. New York, Putnam, 1939.
Lang, Lincoln A.
   Ranching with Roosevelt. Philadelphia, Lippincott, 1926.
Larkin, Margaret
   Singing Cowboy. New York, Knopf, 1931.
Latham, Henry
   Trans-Missouri Stock Raising: the Pasture Lands of North America. Omaha, Daily Herald Steam Printing House, 1871.
Lavender, David S.
   One Man's West. New York, Doubleday, 1943.
Leech, Harper and Carroll, John C.
   Armour and His Times. New York, Appleton-Century, 1938.
Leigh, William R.
   The Western Pony. New York, Huntington Press, 1933.
Lewis, Alfred Henry
   Wolfville. New York, Stokes, 1897.
Lockwood, Frank C.
   Arizona Characters. Los Angeles, Times-Mirror Press, 1928.
Lomax, John A.
   Songs of the Cattle Trail and Cow Camps. New York, Macmillan, 1919.
Long, Richard M.
   Wichita, 1866-1883. Wichita, Kansas, McCormick-Armstrong Company, 1945.
McCarty, John L.
   Maverick Town, the Story of Old Tascosa. Norman, University of Oklahoma Press, 1946.

259

McCauley, James Emmitt
Stove-up Cowboy's Story. Austin, Texas Folklore Society, 1943.

McCoy, Joseph G.
Historic Sketches of the Cattle Trade. Edited by Ralph P. Bieber. Glendale, Calif., A. H. Clark, 1940.

McCoy, Joseph G.
Historic Sketches of the Cattle Trade of the West and Southwest. Kansas City, Missouri, Ramsey, Millett & Hudson, 1874.

McDonald, James
Food from the Far West. London, Nimmo, 1878.

Mackay, Malcolm S.
Cow Range and Hunting Trail. New York, Putnam, 1925.

McNeal, T. A.
When Kansas was Young. New York, Macmillan, 1922.

Majors, Alexander
Seventy Years on the Frontier. Chicago, Rand McNally, 1893.

Marshall, James
Santa Fe: the Railroad That Built an Empire. New York, Random House, 1945.

Mercer, Asa Shinn
The Banditti of the Plains, or The Cattlemen's Invasion of Wyoming. San Francisco, Grabhorn Press, 1935.

Miles, Nelson A.
Personal Recollections and Observations. Chicago, Werner, 1896.

Miles, Nelson A.
Serving the Republic. New York, Harper, 1911.

Miller, Benjamin S.
Ranching in the Southwest. New York, privately printed, 1896.

Missouri, Kansas and Texas Railroad
Reports and Statements. St. Louis, 1879.

Monaghan, Jay
Last of the Bad Men, Tom Horn. Indianapolis, Bobbs-Merrill, 1946.

Montana Stock Grower's Association
Brand Book. Helena, 1885.

Mora, Joseph J.
Californios, the Saga of the Hard-Riding Vaqueros, America's First Cowboys. Garden City, N. Y., Doubleday, 1949.

Mora, Joseph J.
Trail Dust and Saddle Leather. New York, Scribners, 1946.

Myers, John M.
The Last Chance: Tombstone's Early Years. New York, Dutton, 1950.

Myrick, Herbert
Cache la Poudre: the Romance of a Tenderfoot in the Days of Custer. New York, Orange Judd, 1905.

Nimmo, Joseph
The Range and Ranch Cattle Business of the United States. Washington, Government Printing Office, 1885. (Also published as *House Exec. Doc. 7,* Part III, 48th Congress, 2nd session.)

Nordyke, Lewis R.
Cattle Empire: the Fabulous Story of the 3,000,000 Acre XIT. New York, Morrow, 1949.

North, Escott
Saga of the Cowboy. London, Jerrolds, 1942.

Noyes, Alva J.
In the Land of Chinook. Helena, Montana, State Publishing Co., 1917.

O'Beirne, Harry F.
The Indian Territory: Its Chief Legislators and Leading Men. St. Louis, Woodward, 1892.

O'Keefe, Rufus
Cowboy Life. San Antonio, Naylor, 1936.

Olmstead, Frederick Law
A Journey Through Texas. New York, Mason Brothers, 1859.

O'Reilly, Harrington
Fifty Years on the Trail. New York, F. Warne, 1889.

Osgood, Ernest S.
The Day of the Cattleman. Minneapolis, University of Minnesota Press, 1929.

Otero, Miguel A.
My Life on the Frontier. New York, Press of the Pioneers, 1935-1939.

Otero, Miguel A.
The Real Billy the Kid. New York, R. R. Wilson, 1936.

Owen, John
The Journals and Letters of Major John Owen, Pioneer of the Northwest, 1850-1871. Edited by Paul C. Philips. New York, Eberstadt, 1927.

Paine, Albert Bigelow
Captain Bill MacDonald, Texas Ranger. New York, Little & Ives, 1909.

Parrish, Randall
The Great Plains. Chicago, McClurg, 1907.

Paxson, Frederick Logan
History of the American Frontier. New York, Houghton, 1924.

Paxson, Frederick Logan
   The Last American Frontier. New York, Macmillan, 1910.
Peake, Ora Brooks
   The Colorado Range Cattle Industry. Glendale, California, A. H. Clark, 1937.
Pelzer, Louis
   The Cattlemen's Frontier. Glendale, California, A. H. Clark, 1936.
Poe, John W.
   The Death of Billy the Kid. Boston, Houghton, 1933.
Pollock, J. M.
   The Unvarnished West: Ranching as I Found It. London, Simpkin, Marshall, 1911.
Ponting, Tom Candy
   Life of Tom Candy Ponting. Decatur, Illinois, 1904.
Porter, Robert P.
   The West: from the Census of 1880. Chicago, Rand McNally, 1882.
Post, C. C.
   Ten Years a Cowboy. Chicago, McClurg, 1886.
Potter, Jack M.
   Cattle Trails of the Old West. Clayton, New Mexico, Laura H. Krehbiel, 1939.
Potter, Jack M.
   Lead Steer and Other Tales. Clayton, New Mexico, n.d.
Powell, Cuthbert
   Twenty Years of Kansas City's Live Stock Trade and Traders. Kansas City, Missouri, Pearl Printing Company, 1893.
Powell, John W.
   Report on the Lands of the Arid Regions of the United States. Washington, U. S. Interior Department, 1879.
Price, Con
   Trails I Rode. Pasadena, California, Trail's End Publishing Co., 1947.
Prose and Poetry of the Live Stock Industry of the United States, with Outlines of the Origin and Ancient History of Our Live Stock Animals. Volume One (no others published). Denver and Kansas City, National Live Stock Historical Association, 1905.
Raine, William MacLeod
   Famous Sheriffs and Western Outlaws. New York, Doubleday, 1929.
Raine, William MacLeod
   Guns of the Frontier. Boston, Houghton, 1940.
Raine, William MacLeod and Barnes, Will C.
   Cattle. New York, Doubleday, 1930.

Rainey, Mrs. George
   Cherokee Strip Brands. Enid, Oklahoma, 1949.
Rak, Mary Kidder
   A Cowman's Wife. Boston, Houghton, 1934.
Rak, Mary Kidder
   Mountain Cattle. Boston, Houghton, 1936.
Remington, Frederic
   Crooked Trails. New York, Harper, 1898.
Remington, Frederic
   Done in the Open. New York, Russell, 1902.
Remington, Frederic
   Drawings. New York, Russell, 1897.
Remington, Frederic
   Pony Tracks. New York, Harper, 1895.
Rhodes, Eugene Manlove
   Good Men and True. New York, Holt, 1910.
Richthofen, Walter von
   Cattle Raising on the Plains of North America. New York, Appleton, 1885.
Ricketts, William P.
   Fifty Years in the Saddle. Sheridan, Wyoming, Star Publishing Co., 1942.
Ridings, Sam P.
   The Chisholm Trail, a History of the World's Greatest Cattle Trail. Guthrie, Oklahoma, Co-operative Publishing Co., 1936.
Riegel, Robert Edgar
   Story of the Western Railroads. New York, Macmillan, 1926.
Rister, Carl C.
   No Man's Land. Norman, University of Oklahoma Press, 1948.
Rister, Carl C.
   The Southwestern Frontier. Cleveland, A. H. Clark, 1928.
Rollins, Philip Ashton
   The Cowboy, His Characteristics, His Equipment. New York, Scribners, 1922.
Rollinson, John K.
   Hoofprints of a Cowboy and a U. S. Ranger. Caldwell, Idaho, Caxton, 1941.
Rollinson, John K.
   Wyoming Cattle Trails. Caldwell, Idaho, Caxton, 1948.
Rolt-Wheeler, Francis W.
   A Book of Cowboys. Boston, Lothrop, 1921.
Roosevelt, Theodore
   Hunting Trips of a Ranchman. New York, Putnam, 1885.
Roosevelt, Theodore
   Ranch Life and the Hunting Trail. New York, Century, 1888.

Rush, Oscar
The Open Range. Caldwell, Idaho, Caxton, 1936.

Rusling, James Fowler
The Railroads! the Stockyards! the Eveners! an Expose of the Railroad Ring. Washington, R. O. Polkinhorn, 1878.

Russell, Charles M.
Good Medicine. Garden City, N. Y., Garden City Publishing Co., 1936.

Russell, Charles M.
More Rawhides. Great Falls, Montana, Montana Newspaper Association, 1925.

Russell, Charles M.
Rawhide Rawlins Stories. Great Falls, Montana, Montana Newspaper Association, 1921.

Russell, Charles M.
Studies of Western Life. New York, Albertype Company, 1890.

Russell, Charles M.
Trails Plowed Under. Garden City, N. Y., Doubleday, 1928.

Rye, Edgar
The Quirt and the Spur, Vanishing Shadows of the Texas Frontier. Chicago, W. B. Conkey, 1909.

Sage, Lee
The Last Rustler. Boston, Little, Brown, 1930.

Sanders, Alvin H.
Cattle of the World. Washington, National Geographic Society, 1926.

Sanders, Alvin H.
Shorthorn Cattle. Chicago, Sanders, 1901.

Sanders, Alvin H.
Story of the Herefords. Chicago, Breeders' Gazette, 1914.

Santee, Ross
Cowboy. New York, Grossett and Dunlap, 1928.

Santee, Ross
Men and Horses. New York, Century, 1926.

Schatz, August H.
Opening of a Cow Country. Ann Arbor, Edwards Brothers, 1939.

Seely, Howard
A Lone Star Bo-peep, and Other Tales of Texan Ranch Life. New York, W. L. Mershon, 1885.

Shepherd, William
Prairie Experiences in Handling Cattle and Sheep. New York, Orange Judd. 1885.

Siringo, Charlie
Riata and Spurs. Boston, Houghton, 1927.

Siringo, Charlie
A Texas Cowboy. Chicago, Umdenstock & Company, 1885.

Smalley, Eugene Virgil
History of the Northern Pacific Railroad. New York, Putnam, 1883.

Smythe, William E.
Conquest of Arid America. New York, Macmillan, 1905.

Sowell, Andrew Jackson
Rangers and Pioneers of Texas. San Antonio, Shepard Brothers, 1884.

Spring, Agnes Wright
Seventy Years, a Panoramic History of the Wyoming Stock Growers' Association. Cheyenne, 1943.

Stanley, Clark
True Life in the Far West, by the American Cowboy. Worcester, Massachusetts, Musinger Printing Co., n.d.

Stansbery, Lon R.
The Passing of 3-D Ranch. Tulsa, Oklahoma, G. W. Henry, 1930.

Stanton, G. Smith
When the Wildwood was in Flower . . . Fifteen Years Experiences of a Stockman. New York, J. S. Ogilvie, 1909.

Steedman, Charles J.
Bucking the Sage Brush. New York, Putnam, 1904.

Steinel, A. T. and Working, D. W.
History of Agriculture in Colorado. Fort Collins, State Agriculture College, 1926.

Stone, Arthur
Following Old Trails. Missoula, Montana, M. J. Elrod, 1913.

Stout, Tom
Montana, Its Story and Biography. Chicago, American Historical Society, 1921.

Strahorn, Robert E.
The Handbook of Wyoming and Guide to the Black Hills and Big Horn Regions for Citizen, Emigrant and Tourist. Cheyenne, Knight & Leonard, 1877.

Strahorn, Robert E.
The Resources of Montana Territory. Helena, Montana, 1879.

Strand, J.
Memories of Old Western Trails in Texas Longhorn Days. Willeston, North Dakota, Interstate Press, 1931.

Streeter, Floyd B.
Prairie Trails and Cow Towns. Boston, Chapman and Grimes, 1936.

Stuart, Granville
Forty Years on the Frontier. Paul C. Philips, editor. Cleveland, A. H. Clark, 1925.

Stuart, Granville
Montana As It Is. New York, Westcott, 1865.

Sturmberg, Robert
History of San Antonio and of the Early Days in Texas. San Antonio, Standard Printing Company, 1920.

Sullivan, John H.
Life and Adventures of Broncho John; His Second Trip Up the Trail. Valparaiso, Indiana, 1908.

Sullivan, John H.
Life and Adventures of the Original and Genuine Cowboys, by Broncho John. Valparaiso, Indiana, 1905.

Sullivan, W. John L.
Twelve Years in the Saddle for Law and Order. Austin, Texas, Von Boeckmann-Jones Co., 1909.

Sutley, Zack T.
The Last Frontier. New York, Macmillan, 1930.

Sutton, Fred E. and MacDonald, A. B.
Hands Up! Stories of the Six-Gun Fighters of the Old Wild West. Indianapolis, Bobbs-Merrill, 1927.

Sweet, Alexander E. and Knox, J. Armoy
On a Mexican Mustang Through Texas. Hartford, S. S. Scranton, 1883.

Swenson Brothers
The Story of the S M S Ranch. Stamford, Texas, 1919.

Swift, Louis F.
The Yankee of the Yards; the Biography of Gustavus Franklin Swift. Chicago, A. W. Shaw, 1937.

Swisher, James
How I Know; or Sixteen Years on the Western Frontier. Cincinnati, Ohio, The Author, 1881.

Taylor, Thomas U.
Chisholm Trail and Other Routes. San Antonio, Naylor, 1936.

Thayer, William M.
Marvels of the New West. Norwich, Connecticut, Henry Bill Publishing Company, 1887.

Thoburn, Joseph B.
Standard History of Oklahoma. Chicago, American Historical Society, 1916.

Thompson, Albert W.
They Were Open Range Days. Denver, World Press, 1946.

Thompson, George G.
Bat Masterson; the Dodge City Years. Fort Hays, Kansas State College (Language and Literature Series, No. 1), 1943.

Thorp, N. Howard (Jack)
Songs of the Cowboys. Boston, Houghton, 1921.

Thorp, N. Howard (Jack) and Clark, N. M.
Pardner of the Wind. Caldwell, Idaho, Caxton, 1945.

Thrall, Homer S.
A Pictorial History of Texas. St. Louis, Thompson, 1879.

Topping, E. S.
Chronicles of the Yellowstone. St. Paul, Pioneer Press Co., 1883.

Townshend, Richard B.
A Tenderfoot in New Mexico. New York, Dodd Mead, 1924.

Treadwell, Edward F.
The Cattle King. New York, Macmillan, 1931.

Trenholm, Virginia Cole
Footprints on the Frontier. Douglas, Wyoming, Douglas Enterprise Co., 1945.

Triggs, J. H.
History of Cheyenne and Northern Wyoming. Omaha, Herald Publishing Company, 1876.

Trottman, Nelson
History of the Union Pacific. New York, Ronald Press, 1923.

Turner, Frederick Jackson
The Frontier in American History. New York, Holt, 1920.

Twitchell, Ralph Emerson
Leading Facts of New Mexican History. Cedar Rapids, Iowa, Torch Press, 1911-1917.

Wallace, Charles
Mrs. Nat Collins, the Cattle Queen of Montana. St. James, Minnesota, C. W. Foote, 1894.

Walsh, C. C.
Early Days on the Western Range. Boston, Sherman, French and Co., 1917.

Walsh, Richard J.
The Making of Buffalo Bill. Indianapolis, Bobbs-Merrill, 1928.

Walters, Lorenzo D.
Tombstone's Yesterdays. Tucson, Arizona, 1928.

Webb, Walter Prescott
The Great Plains. Boston, Ginn, 1931.

Webb, Walter Prescott
The Texas Rangers. Boston, Houghton, 1935.

Wellman, Paul I.
The Trampling Herd. New York, Carrick & Evans, 1939.

Wendt, Lloyd and Kogan, Herman
Bet a Million! the Story of John W. Gates. Indianapolis, Bobbs-Merrill, 1948.

Wheeler, Homer W.
Buffalo Days; Forty Years in the Old West; the Personal Narrative of a Cattleman. Indianapolis, Bobbs-Merrill, 1925.

Wheeler, Homer W.
The Frontier Trail. Los Angeles, Times-Mirror Press, 1923.

White, Owen P.
Lead and Likker. New York, Minton, Balch, 1932.

White, Owen P.
Them Was the Days. New York, Minton, Balch, 1925.

White, Owen P.
Trigger Fingers. New York, Putnam, 1926.

Williams, J. E.
Fifty-eight Years in the Panhandle of Texas. Austin, Texas, privately printed, 1944.

Wilson, Mrs. Augustus
Memorial Sketch and Official Report of the First National Convention of Cattlemen, November 17-22, 1884. St. Louis, McCoy, 1884.

Wilson Parson's Memorial and Historical Library Magazine, containing scenes and incidents, etc. of the First National Cattlegrower's Convention. St. Louis, 1885.

Wilstach, Frank J.
Wild Bill Hickok, the Prince of Pistoleers. Garden City, N. Y., Doubleday, Page, 1926.

Winslow, Edith Black
In Those Days. San Antonio, Naylor, 1950.

Wister, Owen
The Virginian. New York, Macmillan, 1925.

Wright, Robert M.
Dodge City, the Cowboy Capital. Wichita, Kansas, Wichita Eagle Press, 1913.

II. PERIODICALS, REPORTS, AND OTHER SERIALS

Agricultural History
American Agriculturist
American Cattle Producer
Annals of Iowa
Annals of Wyoming
Breeders' Gazette
Cattleman
Chicago Board of Trade, Annual Reports
Chronicles of Oklahoma
Colorado Farmer and Livestock Journal
Denver Board of Trade, Annual Reports
Frontier Times
Illinois State Historical Society, Journal
Illinois State Historical Society, Publications
Iowa Journal of History and Politics
Kansas City Stockyards, Receipts and Shipments of Livestock
Kansas Farmer
Kansas Historical Quarterly
Kansas State Board of Agriculture, Reports
Kansas State Historical Society, Biennial Reports
Matador Land and Cattle Company, Annual Reports
Mississippi Valley Historical Review
Montana Board of Live Stock Commissioners, Annual Reports
Montana Historical Society, Contributions
National Cattle Growers' Association of America, Proceedings

National Livestock Journal
Nebraska History
Nebraska State Board of Agriculture, Annual Reports
Nebraska State Historical Society, Publications
New Mexico Historical Review
North Dakota Historical Quarterly
North Dakota State Historical Society, Collections
Northwestern Live Stock Journal
Omaha Board of Trade, Annual Reports
Outing Magazine
Panhandle-Plains Historical Review
Prairie Farmer
Rocky Mountain Husbandman
South Dakota Historical Collections
Southwestern Historical Quarterly
Swan Land and Cattle Company, Annual Reports
Union Stockyard and Transit Company, Annual Reports
Union Stockyard and Transit Company, Receipts and Shipments of Livestock
United States Bureau of Animal Industry, Annual Reports
United States Commissioner of Patents, Annual Reports
United States Department of Agriculture, Annual Reports